AIRPORTS ARE
FOR WAITING

AIRPORTS ARE FOR WAITING

And Other Traveler's Tales

Doris Friedensohn

Full Court Press
Englewood Cliffs, New Jersey

Published in the United States of America
by Full Court Press, 601 Palisade Avenue
Englewood Cliffs, NJ 07632
fullcourtpress.com

ISBN 978-1-946989-22-2
Library of Congress Catalog No. 2018966314

*Cover art—"Delayed Flight," 1990, oil on canvas, 78"x90" (front),
and "Waiting," 1990, oil on canvas, 60"x84" (back)—by Elias Friedensohn*

Editing and book design by Barry Sheinkopf

FOR PAUL LAUTER

ACKNOWLEDGMENTS

This small book spans more than a half century of travel—in Africa, Asia, the Middle East, Europe, and the Americas (including Alaska and Puerto Rico). It's a pleasure here to acknowledge many debts and my heartfelt thanks to a long list of special colleagues, companions and friends.

But first a word about essays in the drawer and my publisher, Barry Sheinkopf at Full Court Press (Englewood Cliffs, NJ). At the end of a trip to Vietnam in late March 2018, I banged out some reactions, sent the piece to family and friends, and read it to my writers' group. Then I filed it away in a flashy-looking box with other unpublished travel pieces. A few days later, I wrote to Barry with a proposal for what soon became *Airports are for Waiting and Other Traveler's Tales*. His attentiveness and experience made the publishing process almost pain-free.

Like many travelers, I've been incredibly lucky with my timing and friends. In 1976, the U.S. Department of State funded a series of international conferences to mark the Bicentennial of the United States. I was at the time Vice-President of the American Studies Association (ASA), known mostly for my work with the Connections Collective, advocating multiculturalism, student-centered teaching, and a critical view of U.S. imperialism. When we heard about the Bicentennial meetings, Alice Kessler-Harris put the State Department organizer on the spot. "Who are the women you'll be sending?" she asked. Alice's query got me to the Ivory Coast in 1976. Many extraordinary opportunities followed.

I mention this moment first to salute Alice, a Connections

pal, for deftly flying the feminist flag back then and for decades of talk thereafter about women, American Studies, and learning from travel. But I also want to acknowledge a shift in outlook on gender in the ASA and at the U.S. Information Agency, which sponsored those meetings around the world. Yes, American women belonged on international academic programs and could serve as consultants to colleagues abroad; we had no special fear of flying. At USIA, to my delight, Les High, Bill Bate and Paul Hiemstra—among others—kept communications open, easy, and straightforward.

Special thanks go to Ronald Clifton and his wife Gwili. Ron was Cultural Affairs Officer in Tunisia during my Fulbright year (1978–79); and he held the same post in Ireland when I visited in 1985. Parties at the Cliftons were genial affairs—opportunities to meet scholars, journalists, bankers, and artists. Ron went on to become the Director of Programs in American Studies at the Salzburg Seminar (Salzburg, Austria), where he invited me on several occasions to lecture and also to enjoy a two-month stint as Scholar in Residence. At the Seminar I met a number of engaging foreign scholars—including Eva Valentova from the Czech Republic, Elzbieta Oleksy from Poland, and Nabil Alawi from Palestine —who subsequently invited me to visit their institutions. I'm grateful to Marty Gecek, Ron Clifton's deputy, who later took over the leadership of the Seminar's American Studies Programs, for her spirited work and for keeping me involved in Seminar doings.

Among the special connections of the Fulbright year in Tunisia was the friendship my husband Eli and I developed with Ben and Mary Ann Whitten. Ben was the U.S. embassy librarian, and Mary Ann worked with the Department of English at the University of

Tunis, advising them on library holdings. Mary Ann's subsequent State Department assignment to UNESCO in Paris opened the door to exhibiting *Generations of Women* there. I'm forever grateful to my Jersey City State College colleague and dear friend Barbara Rubin for the partnership leading to this exhibit and the book that followed. What a fine time we had, year after year, lunching at Laiko's, getting giddy on Scotch and cunning at grant-writing.

A second Fulbright, to Portugal in 1985, cemented the decades-long friendship I've relished with Maria Irene Ramalho de Sousa Santos, Chair of the Department of English and American Literature at the University of Coimbra. Thanks to Irene, I've returned to Portugal a half dozen times for talks, conferences and the wonders of suckling pig, *bacalao* and *vinho verde*.

I've written at length about both Fulbrights (especially in *Eating as I Go: Scenes from America and Abroad*, University Press of Kentucky, 2005), but the pieces here on both places are new. The same is true for discussions of Georgia and Mexico and my "Post Cards" from Mozambique and Nepal. I note that several essays, revised for this book, first appeared in *Women on Campus*, a publication of Women's Studies and The Women's Center at Jersey City State College (now New Jersey City University). A special thank-you goes to the late William Reopell, JCSC Director of Publications, for very generously supporting what others might have dismissed as a peripheral endeavor; and to Ellen Wayman-Gordon, Director of the JCSC Office of Public Information, for steadfastly promoting our feminist activities, publications, and projects. Warmest thanks also to the late William J. Maxwell and to Carlos Hernandez, past Presidents of JCSC, for their friendship and lively interest in my travels.

Over the years, I've taken trips with many close friends—only a few of whom are mentioned by name in these pieces. I'm especially grateful for the company and wisdom of Barbara Rubin, Ferris Olin, Delight Dodyk, Adelaide Reyes, Nancy Melzer, Batya Monder, Marilyn Halter, my cousin Caryl Ratner, and my stepdaughter, Shola Friedensohn. In 2013 I traveled to Mexico with Friends of Oaxacan Folk Art (FOFA); *mil gracias* to Arden Rothstein, Deborah Huntington, Joyce Grossbart, Amy Mulvihill, Margee Rogers, Cindy Weill, Lucy Atkin, and Otto Peron for their company and responses to the work of some remarkable young folk artists.

Several of these essays are inspired by the cultural interests and enthusiasms of my late husband, Elias Friedensohn. Eli, a painter and professor of art, resonated to artistic distinction, craftsmanship, hidden histories, and quirky talent. I relished his passion and hoped one day to acquire some measure of his playfulness with ideas.

After Eli's death in 1991, I shared endless travel observations via email with my California colleague on the American Studies circuit, Stanley Bailis. Emails to Stan were indispensable in reconstructing several trips reported on here. I can't thank him enough for tolerating my meanderings and for his readiness to read me critically.

Other discerning readers have protected me from platitudes, long-windedness, and complacency. I'm grateful to Rachel Brownstein, Blair Birmelin, and Rita Jacobs for their candor and discerning criticism over many decades. My thanks, too, to the members of my writers' group—Marc Bernstein, Joseph Chuman, Theresa Forsman, and Patricia LeFevre—for twenty years (how amazing!) of close attention to words and ideas.

In 2016 I responded to a call for essays on being a widow. My piece, "Losing the Artist, Living with His Work" (in *Widows' Words*, edited by Nan Bauer-Maglin, Rutgers University Press, 2019), led to more intimate ways of writing about Eli's art. That impulse lives in some of these pieces—and in my revisions of earlier versions.

I've been hugely fortunate, over the past six years, to live and vacation with a rare American Studies colleague and partner: a man who can adjust with equal aplomb to non-stop traffic in Ho Chi Minh City, subways without English signage in Tokyo, and six-foot Heliconia resembling birds-at-rest in Costa Rica. Paul Lauter, whom I first met on the Women's Studies circuit in the early 1980s (while he was promoting publications of The Feminist Press and I was exhibiting *Generation of Women*), is an indefatigable traveler. I tag after him to oddball museums, nature preserves, symphony halls, and fine restaurants, too. He locates one-of-a-kind hotels, wacky gift shops, and my elusive email on his laptop computer. Paul's sweet, loving company keeps me balanced on the road —even when I'm yearning for a print copy of the *New York Times* at my own dining room table. This book is for him.

—D.F.,
December 2018

TABLE OF CONTENTS

❖

INTRODUCTION

MARCH 2018: ON THE LAST LEG of our flight back from Vietnam, I check my watch and do some fast math: twenty-eight hours since we left the hotel in Hoi An, three flights, five hours of dead time in the old Saigon Airport, three hours lost in a diversion for a medical emergency somewhere near Reykjavik—and still another two hours to JFK. Then waiting for the bags, lining up at Customs, and watching anxiously for our limo before crawling along the Van Wyck Expressway and over the GWB. The body rebels, and the psyche deflates. Crankiness out-muscles common sense. I write in a notebook, *This is the end of world travel for me.*

Whether it is actually the end or not isn't the issue. It's the intensity of those feelings that interests me. After fifty years of frequent flying—outside of the continental U.S. and often to exotic Third World locations—I am losing my appetite for adventure. Let me rephrase this: Perhaps what I'm losing is my tolerance for frustration. What's happened to my flexibility? Sense of humor? Curiosity? Perspective? How do I account for feeling so grouchy and entitled?

Some good habits, I'm relieved to report, remain constant. Two days after returning to Leonia, I'm at my desk, trying to make sense of my encounter with Vietnam. As I review my notes, hand-written and in emails, I observe that (as is my habit) many important sites go unremarked—along with many noteworthy meals. Why mimic the guidebook? More and more as a traveler, I'm watching myself respond: watching the play of my curiosity and wariness, my openness and indifference. Confronting ten lanes of traffic (and almost no traffic lights) in Vietnamese cities, I react with fear and frustration—and then semi-repressed anger. One shouldn't need a tour bus and a local tour guide to halt the flood of those cars and motorbikes so that we can approach the War Remnants Museum (formerly known as the Museum of American Atrocities), the historic Ben Thanh Market for textiles and crafts, or the Jade Emperor Pagoda, where vendors sell live turtles carrying blessings. But we do. Okay, forget casual walking in Ho Chi Minh City (formerly Saigon) and Hanoi.

These constraints in Vietnam trigger re-considerations of walking back home, in New York. Along with some eight million who live in the city or use it regularly, I walk (and drive) amid double buses, an armada of trucks delivering online purchases, and a hundred thousand newly licensed Ubers, Lyfts, and other limos. I dodge among the blue rental bikes and the scooters, the red construction cones, the plastic bags of garbage, and all those pedestrians focused on their smart phones. Traveling, I remind myself, illuminates "here" as well as "there."

This collection of travel essays—all reporting on experiences outside of the continental U.S.—spans the early 1960s to the present moment. While I have published travel pieces in academic journals and in my food memoir, *Eating as I Go: Scenes from America and Abroad* (University Press of Kentucky, 2005), most of the Traveler's Tales found here are written for this collection. A few pieces, considerably revised, first appeared in *Women on Campus* and other publications of Jersey City State College (now New Jersey City University).

Often on these pages, I'm reflecting on a stint as a specialist/scholar of American culture. Often, I'm bringing "news" about contemporary America (politics, racial tensions, and feminism in particular). For trips to Tunisia, Portugal, Guinea, Georgia, the Czech Republic, Japan, Mozambique, and Argentina, I'm indebted to U.S. government monies supporting American Studies. In Tunisia and Portugal, I was a Fulbright professor; elsewhere, I enjoyed short-term assignments to attend conferences or to work with international colleagues on teaching about the United States. What unlikely good fortune: Three degrees focused on my own society and culture have morphed into a government-supported passport to world travel!

What about the dark side of the American experience? Imperialism and militarism, for example. Trips to Cuba and Vietnam provide occasions for looking at the cost others pay for U.S. world "leadership" and dominance. In Havana, buildings in deep disrepair suggest a shortage of materials and funds related to the U.S. boycott. In Vietnam, the presence of many crippled adults reminds me that Agent Orange lives on in their bodies and so-called unexploded ordinance continues (fifty years after the end of the war) to explode and maim.

Self-improvement is one of the classic excuses for travel. I've seized opportunities to study Spanish abroad (in Guatemala on multiple occasions) and to attend writers' workshops (in Italy and Mexico). Having done so much teaching as a traveler, I've relished being given assignments and worrying mostly about myself.

Have I mentioned "vacation"? Time off from ordinary American doings? Time to walk under a big sky or swim in warm waters? Trips to Crete and Costa Rica address the pleasures of "escape"— along with a cruise to Alaska, where whales splash and dive while (most) ordinary humans take photos.

The collection opens with a 1962 misadventure entitled "Choices," about traveling to Puerto Rico for an abortion. While the trip preceded my coming to feminism by about a decade, it touches, inevitably, upon women's vulnerability and subordination. I explore these issues more fully in an essay on my Guatemalan Spanish teacher, her sister, and her mother. Feminist conferences lure me to China and Korea; the photo exhibit "Generations of Women," developed with my collaborator Barbara Rubin, at Jersey City State College, is my ticket to France and Ireland.

Traveling, I see myself freshly. The light in a strange locale can be sharper and less forgiving than at home. I see my impatience, mistakes, adaptations, and the judgments I'm quick to make (and sometimes regret); I see the liberties I take as a stranger.

Small moments often tell big stories. Alternating with my regular chapters are fifteen "Post Cards," anecdotes compressed into a three-hundred-word comment. These include accidental meetings and reactions in galleries; lessons from a museum, a synagogue, an office, two hotels, and a hike on a hill; and from "doing American Studies abroad." Friends and family know that I've always had a weakness for post cards, doubtless because I travel without a camera. I let someone else's image of a place provoke my own thirty-word comment in the space provided. I'm drawing a verbal picture, leaving the recipient to wonder what else I might know.

These Post Cards have a similar conceit. I've inserted them without regard for chronology, to stress the moment itself and my personal reaction, and (sometimes) to play against or with the preceding, longer piece. It's a risky strategy, I know. These much-abbreviated experiences are not separate from history. Post Cards like "The Documentation Center" (in Nuremberg, Germany) and "The Jews of Djerba" (in Tunisia) evoke matters of enormous political significance and cultural complexity. I mean no disrespect in being so brief.

In the first essay, "Choices," I'm alone. In subsequent pieces, I travel with my late husband Eli, with my partner Paul, and occasionally with women friends. I team up with my stepdaughter Shola in Cuba and Hawaii; I visit my son Adam in Nepal, where he spent almost two decades running a solar energy business and studying Buddhism. For twenty-one years after Eli's death in 1991, I'm often on my own—frequently "on assignment." Alone, I develop a heightened awareness of places and spaces, opportunities and vulnerabilities. Alone, I'm more open and more careful. While I crave stimulation, I rarely seek intimacy.

Writing, I press myself to confront what did and did not happen—and occasionally why something could have happened but didn't. At the end of a trip, recounting the latest adventure over drinks with friends, I'm given to exaggeration and, occasionally, to silly rhapsodizing. Writing is a corrective: a chance for more subtlety and maybe (just maybe) more honesty, too.

My house contains a visual record of these travels: my husband's paintings, African masks, Mexican ceramics, Tunisian oil lamps, Turkish rugs, Nepalese fabrics, Guatemalan place mats, Portuguese bowls, and Japanese chopsticks—along with photographs, books, old calendars, and four sets of hanging postcards, which are my birthday presents to Paul. The pieces collected on these pages don't catch the morning light, and they don't enhance the rituals of dining. But they do remind me of how I learn and what I value—and why traveling matters.

CHOICES: PUERTO RICO AND PREGNANT, 1962

C *LARO QUE SI,"* I SAY, LETTING THE WORDS flow with just enough rhythm and speed. *"Me encanto hablar espanol."* I look up and smile at the man with seductive dark eyes and a perfectly groomed mustache who is peering into my vagina. My feet are in stirrups, a rough yellow sheet covers my body, and I am flirting in Spanish with an obstetrician who is performing a D & C on me.

It's 1962 at a small maternity clinic in San Juan, Puerto Rico. I'm in trouble, in a strange place, and at the mercy of an unknown physician. Concentrating on Spanish, I attempt to block out the humiliations that have led me to the clinic and the spasms of pain from the doctor's scraping. Across the barriers of culture and assigned doctor–patient roles, I turn on whatever charm I can muster.

I FLEW INTO INTO SAN JUAN (only four hours from LaGuardia) yesterday afternoon feeling oddly excited. No one I know has taken this journey, and close friends will be avid for anecdotes: How did I manage alone? How did I feel? How was PR? My arrival was uncomplicated, I'll tell them. No passport to show. No money to change. After checking into a modest downtown hotel, I wandered out for a glance at the cathedral, the statue of Ponce de Leon, and the city hall. I remember nothing about those landmarks (of course, there are pictures in my guide book) except the cobblestones under my feet and the hot, humid air at 6:00 p.m. At a small restaurant on the Plaza —was it called la Galina?—I ordered *arroz con pollo* and a *cerveza*. Afterwards, in my silent, windowless room, I slept for eight hours.

The next morning, I'll report, after a *café con leche* in the hotel's breakfast room, I returned to the cobblestones. I bought four postcards of San Juan from a distracted woman guarding the sidewalk stand, peered into a cafeteria full of elderly men, and observed a crowd waiting patiently at a bus stop. For forty minutes I ambled around, straining to catch snippets of conversation. Then, consulting my map, I located the unpaved street leading to Dr. A.'s clinic.

The receptionist at the front desk greeted me warmly and complimented me on my Spanish. Dr. A., she said, had been called to Philadelphia, and his associate, Dr. E., would take care of me. Three faded blue couches with oversized, print-covered cushions filled the waiting room. Tall palms in painted orange pots caressed the ceiling. Several huge-bellied women ambled around, chattering loudly in Spanish. Glancing at the unswept floor and dust-covered windows, I wondered briefly about the level of housekeeping in the operating room.

I will never know whether it was my success in distracting Dr. E. from his surgical procedures, his ineptitude, or the unsanitary conditions in the clinic that caused *el medico* to botch the job. But botch it he did. Two days later, I left Puerto Rico with a murderous headache and forebodings of trouble to come. I returned to graduate school in New Haven, hemorrhaging heavily and writhing in pain. Shortly thereafter, I was admitted to Grace New Haven Hospital, where a second, legal and sterile D&C was performed. The surgery was legal because I was infected and seriously ill. The obstetrician who performed it had advised me two months earlier—when confirming that I was indeed pregnant—"to marry your young man as soon as possible."

In some respects, mine is a familiar story. I had a diaphragm but was careless in using it. The night I conceived, the diaphragm was in place, but I failed to check it to be sure it was in correctly. I recall that we had been arguing that evening and drinking a fair bit of Scotch. Then we moved quickly to bed.

My romance with Steve, in its sixth month, had begun auspiciously: tennis in Central Park on lazy summer afternoons, dinners in chic French bistros in the West 50s, and bedding down in Danish modern motel rooms a few miles north of Riverdale. Of course, I thought I was in love with Steve, and I had reason to believe he was smitten with me. I also knew he had secrets that I was obliged to respect. When it was clear that I was pregnant, Steve offered to help me locate an abortionist—no easy matter when abortion was illegal everywhere in the U.S.—and cover the costs.

With no wedding bells in the offing, I embraced the decision to end my pregnancy. I was twenty-five, a fourth-year graduate student in New Haven anticipating my first, full-time teaching position. Within a week, Steve had located a doctor "in the business" in West New York, New Jersey, across the River from the south end of Central Park. His office, in a nondescript frame house with a half dozen hard wood chairs and a pair of scratched plastic tables, gave off the stench of failure. Dr. C., I decided, was probably a Mafia brother-in-law. I imagined the police breaking down the front door, finding me on the operating table, and hauling us both off to jail. My parents would be called. Yale would be notified. Disgrace seemed a hair's-breadth away.

At that juncture, one of my contacts at Yale Law School recommended Dr. A. in San Juan. He did clean work for North American women, I was assured, and his clinic would never be busted. His fee was $250 to $500, less than Dr. C. was charging in West New York.

ON THE PHONE IN MY ROOM in New Haven's best hospital was a woman with a beautifully modulated voice. The caller identified herself as Steve's wife and the mother of their two young children. Her marriage was coming apart, she said, but she wasn't quite ready to let go—for the children's sake. Would I please leave her husband alone?

I shouldn't have been surprised. Steve's wife confirmed what I already knew or should have known but refused to know. He was a cad, but I was a fool. I hung up the phone in a daze.

Steve pleaded for forgiveness. He assured me that he planned to leave his wife as soon as details could be worked out, but I wasn't interested.

Two months later, I accepted a position in the English Department of the University of Vermont, eight hours by car from Metropolitan New York and Steve. By the time I moved to Burlington in August, Steve had also moved—to an apartment of his own. But I was set on a new course and hoped never to hear from him again.

AN AFTERWORD: IT IS HUMBLING TO BE SO STUPID in love, to feel trapped by sexual chemistry and the yearning for intimacy. But one trap need not lead to another. Even in 1962, I knew I had choices; and I am grateful to this day that I had the cash and connections to take advantage of them. The personal is political, we keep reminding ourselves; we dare not forget the lesson. With the memory of Dr. A.'s clinic and Grace New Haven Hospital still fresh in my mind—more than a half century later—I reach for my checkbook several times a year. I sign endless petitions, march when I can, and support only pro-Choice candidates. My good fortune must be every woman's right.

POST CARD: MASKS OF ROSE D'IVOIRE, IVORY COAST, 1976

I WATCH *Eli surveying African masks on the walls of Rose d'Ivoire, an art gallery in the fanciest hotel in Abidjan. It's our last day in the Ivory Coast, the end of an ambitious but "complicated" conference on American Studies in Africa. Shopping, we can decompress, make choices, feel in charge.*

Eli positions himself in front of a fierce head with massive hair, bulging eyes, and nails for teeth. From Niger, according to the label. War has been declared, the mask announces, and this rage-filled male is leading the assault. My husband points at the fellow and smiles. "No, I don't think so," I say hesitantly. His judgment, I know, has been shaped by decades of museum visits, reading art history, painting, and occasional forays into sculpture.

"Fierceness personified," Eli comments. "He's territorial, in command, gorgeously willful. Let's take him home."

Home? To Leonia? Where will he reign? And how will I manage my resistance? I scan the walls frantically—until I spot something different: a woman's head (Baole, from the Ivory Coast) with smooth, high cheekbones, wide eyes, and an aura of serenity. "We need her," I tell Eli, "to keep him in check. Perhaps in the center hall—greeting guests, assuring them that balance is beautiful."

We pull out our traveler's checks, his and hers, and arrange for shipment. I imagine our new acquisitions in their separate spaces, speaking war and peace. I imagine passing him on the way to the dining room and passing her on the way to the front door. Perhaps, over time, I'll pay less heed to male rage while I relish the wonder and authority of female restraint. How long will it take, I wonder, to live more easily with him and more richly with her?

NAKED ON STAVROS, CRETE, 1973

O N THE RIGHT EDGE OF A LARGE PAINTING above my desk, I consider a naked version of myself at thirty-five: striding along next to Eli, also naked but wearing a straw hat. My body is firm, my small breasts agreeably enlarged, and my blond hair in a French twist. I'm not looking at Eli, not touching him, but we seem purposeful together. Perhaps we've been discussing the Power of Love or the Nature of Progress. More likely, Eli has been holding forth, as was his habit: lecturing me on Conquest, Ruins, or Human Deviousness. Any of these might account for my unsmiling expression.

This 1973 version of Eli and me at Stavros—on the north coast of Crete—is fixed in paint as well as in memory. The painting, which captures us on vacation, celebrates nature and the body beautiful. In the background, a deep blue sky fills more than half of the canvas. Behind our figures on the right, at about the same height, looms a light-filled, mountainous terrain. On this site, according to legend, Zeus was born and Athena emerged from sparkling blue water. The Minoans built multi-story palaces here and decorated their walls with frescoes. Of course, tourists arrive in droves.

We have rented a large, airy apartment overlooking the Port of Chania, Crete's second city and about twenty minutes from Stavros. The owner, once a teacher of art at the Dalton School in New York, vacationed here some ten years ago and vowed never to leave. Recently, she acquired a small house in the interior, where she retreats when paying guests, often artist friends, visit the island. Each morning, at tall windows overlooking the Port, we watch the sun rise and the fishing boats depart. The scent of rosemary fills the air.

On walks along the water's edge, we chat with restaurant workers and admire the local greens and the fish in small tanks waiting for customers to select them. Our favorite place, with six wooden tables outside, is known for grilled octopus, which we relish, and tomatoes—fresher than any I've ever tasted—in a citrus olive oil. One evening at dinner, we sit next to Greeks eating a (gorgeously) grilled lamb's head. Eli immediately orders one. Indeed, the tastes of the cheeks are magical: crispy, crunchy, meaty, and laced with just enough fat. The lips are equally inviting. But the eyes are another matter. Our Greek neighbors plop them in their mouths, but we hold back. Too weird, at least for today, we tell one another.

Our rented VW bug bounces along on the island's rough roads. I remember coming upon an encampment of European hippies settled in caves and facing a beach. Well oiled, drinking ouzo and smoking pot, they appear to have it all—along with good sex, we assume, come evening. Somehow their freedom and sense of entitlement irritates Eli. Intruders, he calls them. Are we any differ-

ent? I ask. Enjoying a spacious apartment, a summer without ob-
ligations, and two academic salaries? Enjoying these magically blue
skies and clean beaches, along with the freshest salads and a buggy
that's easy on gas?

Stavros is full of hope. Although Eli has painted us looking
grave, we are, in fact, heroic figures in the landscape: not dwarfed
by it nor daunted by the burden of history. What a good omen for
the time just ahead! We are about to settle into a new house in an
unknown town across the George Washington Bridge from the familiar Upper West Side. After the radical freedom of Crete, we'll
confront career responsibilities (including a new job for me), large
ambitions, and the inevitable anxieties. On crowded highways and
at dreary, pointless meetings, we'll lose precious time. Eli will fret
about dampness in the basement, and I'll be cranky fixing dinner.
Surely, we'll long for this Dream, this unencumbered interlude
where nature offers freedom and nakedness implies strength.

POST CARD: ROOM 17, ITALY, 2000

T*HE WHEELS OF MY SUITCASE SQUEAL against the stone floor, shattering the silence of the convent. I had planned to bring the new carry-on bag with better wheels. Then at the last moment, I yielded to the larger version with space for Italian tapes (that I probably won't listen to) and two additional novels (that I probably won't read). With four wheels on the base of the long end, and a soft, makeshift pulley, this familiar traveling companion wiggles and trembles. It's also too scarred from a decade of frequent flying and rough handling (including five trips to Nepal, three to Guatemala, and one each to Guinea and Georgia) ever to interest a thief.*

I ponder the impulse that explains clinging to this battered bag. Neurotic anxiety? Poor packing habits? A need for familiar supports in unfamiliar places? Wishing for the safety of invisibility when, as a very tall woman, I feel so visible?

The suitcase topples over, interrupting my meditation. Righting it, I glance at the number on the door to my right: 17, my room. Seventeen is an "eight" (seven plus one), I can hear my friend Barbara saying. "Eight is an auspicious number." For more than twenty years, whenever Barbara and I have given papers together on feminist teaching or talks on our women's photo-history exhibits, she has regaled me with "readings" based on "the science of numerology." I'm in my eighth year, she told me before I flew to Spoleto. The eighth year, Barbara elaborated, is about power, responsibility, recognition—and ardor for work. I've got a demanding week ahead here at the Spoleto Writer's Workshop. Let's hope the ardor will help.

My key is in the door to Room 17. I can hear the stillness.

CARO DOMENICO: TUNISIA, 1978–79

Caro Domenico,

I remember a wicked rain battering the cobblestones of the medina the night we met. Eli and I raced along rue Djaama ez Zitouna, stopping to kiss in the downpour. We glanced briefly at the famous mosque before embracing again. And again. An old Tunisian woman, wrapped in black and passing within a foot of us, hissed.

In the hallway of Umberto and Mariu's building, I slipped on the marble floor, cursing as I fell. A dozen red roses, our offering for the dinner party to come, escaped from their flimsy wrapping. Domenico, this wasn't an auspicious way to begin an evening. But at least I hadn't sprained an ankle or busted an elbow.

Climbing the stone steps, four flights up to the Cardozos' sprawling, painting-filled flat, I felt my heart pounding from emotional overload: delicious love, suspicious Tunisians, an accident averted, intense new friendships, a *saltimbocca* sizzling on the stove, and whatever surprises the evening might offer.

Our hosts, Umberto and Mariu, had opened their private world to us. Umberto, an Italian Jew from a storied family, had been born in Tunis. Mariu, Italian, Catholic, and also a native Tunisian, had taken on Umberto's outsider (and risk-filled) Jewish identity. Like Eli and me, the Cardozos do not belong to a synagogue; nor do they celebrate "the holidays." But they value Jewish history and the cultural achievements of Jews. In Umberto's youth, Jews and Muslims mixed more easily in Tunis; but since the Yom Kippur War, anti-Semitism has festered. Outsiders like us may not read the signs, but Umberto keeps a low profile. The couple invites only a few special guests to one of Mariu's refined, southern Italian dinners. Muslim friends are elaborately vetted.

I thrust the wounded bouquet at Mariu, wetting her cheeks with my kisses. "Please put the flowers in my son's room," she said in French, our common language. She pointed toward the tidy schoolboy's study, with a notebook and two dictionaries (Arabic-French and French-Italian) on the desk, vacant for ten years since Stefano's death.

Eli stood framed in the doorway to the formal dining room with a Johnny Walker Red, Umberto's scotch of choice, in his left hand. His right hand clasped your left shoulder, Domenico. You laughed till the tears came. What a pair you were: two lean, craggy-faced men with Mediterranean noses and salt-and-pepper hair, both in turtlenecks and corduroys, enjoying the shock of recognition.

"Doris, love," Eli called out. "*Questo Italiano*, who is trying to pass as a New York painter, is Gianni Battista's journalist friend. In Rome, Gianni and I used to drink grappa every evening and smoke expensive Gitanes. The first time that Domenico joined us at Café Due Amici—it was New Year's Day, 1959—Gianni and I got into a nasty fight about whether Braque could hold a candle to Picasso.

"To salvage the evening, Domenico interrogated me about Jackson Pollock; that's how I discovered what a wily fellow he is."

DOMENICO, ELI TURNED FIFTY-FOUR that year in Tunis. We had been together twelve years and were relishing our own Mediterranean heaven: a cottage with a big kitchen, a couple of bedrooms, a modern bathroom, and a huge brick terrace facing the sea. Eli, on sabbatical, had set up an easel in the dining room. I was on a Fulbright, lecturing to more than two hundred students on immigration, multiculturalism, and the (changing) American way of life. A couple of students actually wondered if I worked for the CIA.

Eli painted peasant women carrying wood and water, street life in the souks, the ritual slaughter of sheep, and the enigmas of commerce between the sexes. His canvases of Tunisian couples in love and war exploded with manic wit. I wish you could see *"Elle Veux Trop"* (She Wants Too Much), an oil from that moment hanging in our living room. A Tunisian man and woman, each with a strong presence and a prominent nose, glower at one another. They could be discussing their sleeping arrangements, a daughter's dowry, or how many sheep to sell in the market. Mystery energizes the painting.

Domenico, you told us you had just celebrated the big 5-0, and you wanted us to toast to friendships renewed and lasting love. Stealing a look at my handsome husband—whom I would describe when looking for him on the streets of Tunis as "that man who resembles President Lincoln"—I thought, yes, let us continue to be lucky in love.

You and Eli were like sparring partners in verbal overdrive, both wordsmiths in more than one language. I envied Eli's smooth Italian and his fluent, Parisian French. He'd brought a French grammar with him to Tunis. To stay *au courant*, he read *La Presse* regularly.

Later, in the U.S., when your notes arrived—full of acid comments about our Hollywood President—Eli pored over them, checking every unfamiliar term in his tattered Italian dictionary. He did the equivalent, in French, with Umberto's letters. Your disdain for Hollywood-in-Washington exceeded his own, he reported to me, gleefully.

We never knew, Domenico, that you were a Spoletino. Your TV-perfect Italian and cashmere overcoat, the American directors you preferred to Fellini and Visconti, the stylish haircut that put Eli's to shame—these, and your thirty-year bond with Umberto and Gianni, spelled cosmopolitan and *Romano*.

There's so much that we didn't know about you. And much that you didn't know about us. For example, we had a pro-forma Mexican marriage (convenient in the early '70s when we lived in a small college town in Upstate New York), which had no legal standing in New York. Later, we settled into an early twentieth-century stucco house in a tranquil town in northern New Jersey. We were, in the American way, absorbed by our careers. With exhibits to prepare, articles to write, and classes to teach, we lost contact with you, Domenico. We never visited your apartment in Rome; we never met your son and two daughters. Eli always wondered whether your marriage had survived—and what dark musings compromised your sleep.

I learned about your death when I visited Spoleto in 2000. So strange: during a writers' workshop in that seductive Umbrian town, I stumbled upon your stone in the local cemetery: *Domenico Vissani, 1927–89*. Of course, I wondered how things had ended for you. Was it a heart attack, Domenico? Or a smoker's death? A cancer of the esophagus, perhaps? Like Eli's?

Te amo, fratello mio,

Doris

POST CARD: SIX DEGREES
OF SEPARATION, ARGENTINA, 1977

A PALE, MIDDLE-AGED MAN IN A WELL-CUT *navy suit has been watching Eli and me. We sit, separated by two gray plastic chairs, in the Pan Am departure area. Our flight from Buenos Aires to JFK is thirty minutes late. "You're from New York, by any chance?" he asks, in formal, Spanish-inflected English.*

"New Yorkers, born and bred," Eli says, not quite imagining where this Small World game will go.

"We've just had some excellent doctors, from Mt. Sinai in New York, giving a consultation at my hospital. In neurology. Do you by any chance know the Doctors K.? Such a splendid couple?"

I watch Eli compose a response. "The Doctors K., Howard and Dorothy? Thirty-five years for Dorothy, ever since high school, and a bit less for Howard."

"A remarkable medical couple," the traveling doctor adds. "So wise and so good at working together. Will you be seeing them in New York? Please give them my warmest and most respectful greetings." The doctor hands Eli his card.

Jacobo Mendez de Oro, *it reads. Had he been an infant at*

Ellis Island, I think to myself, he would have become Jake Goldstein.

This isn't the moment to describe the Kriegers' elegant dinner parties—where psychiatrists and neurologists predictably tangle; nor to mention their extensive collection of Eli's paintings. Smiles are enough—and promises to pass along the Argentine's best wishes.

I PHONE DOTTY AS SOON AS WE RETURN *to Leonia and describe our meeting with Dr. Mendez de Oro. "He raved about you and Howard as an amazing team," I say.*

There's a long pause before Dotty responds, "Howard and I are getting divorced. I'm weary of our empty marriage."

ABROAD WITH GENERATIONS OF WOMEN, FRANCE AND IRELAND, 1983

S UNDAY, MARCH 6, 1983. 8:45 A.M. A UNESCO guard ushers us through the deserted building at Place de Fontenoy, unlocks Main Hall, and throws on six banks of lights. *Voilà! Formidable!* I'm looking at an enormous, handsomely furnished art gallery and lounge: a grand site for exhibiting *Generations of Women*. The guard is puzzled. No events are scheduled for Main Hall on March 6. However, he's following instructions: show the site to Ms. Mary Ann Whitten, Cultural Officer for the U.S. Delegation, and her guest from the States.

When Mary Ann and I return twenty-four hours later, Main Hall feels like a global traffic center: People from every continent— UNESCO staff, delegates from member nations, and miscellaneous visitors—are streaming through the space. *Generations of Women* will have a built-in audience. Even those rushing to a meeting will notice the flashing dark eyes and Latin drama of Raquel O'Lear from Panama, the striking presence of Abosede Akande in traditional Nigerian garb, and nineteen-year-old Augusta Schrober and her female companion in a 1918 photo, working as train conductors on the German railroad. I've brought these women, plus another twenty, across the Atlantic for UNESCO's celebration of International Women's Day on March 8. As the poster accompanying the show explains, the subjects are the female forebears of Women's Studies students at Jersey City State College.

With Mary Ann's help, I lay the black-and-white photos (20 x 30" on Styrofoam boards) on the floor, with the narratives (one index card in French, and another in English) next to them. Hanging this show, which my collaborator Barbara Rubin and I have done at least thirty times by now, is hardly an exact science. Big heads usually look well together, and so do family groups and portraits of couples. Often, the shapes and lengths of the walls dictate how the photos are organized. Every exhibit of *Generations* has its own idiosyncratic look.

I'm crouching on the floor next to "Lucia d'Amico and Her Grandchildren" (the two little kids standing on chairs to be at eye level with the weathered old woman) when a man stops to chat. He's an emigre artist, he says, originally from Russia. He has just come upon "The Bushkins of Bialystock" (c. 1900)—Bialystock, where he's from!—and wants the back story. The student who gave us the original (for this enlargement), I tell him, is a sixty-five-year-old woman (yes, sixty-five and getting a B.A. at my college) who grew up in an immigrant Jewish family. The artist examines the Bushkin clan, five adults and four children, all in their finest attire and seated for a formal portrait. While he doesn't know the Bushkins, he says, he has a half dozen family pictures like this one tucked away in an ancient desk in his studio.

Five minutes later, an Indian, pointing to a photo of the Prabhu family from Pilar in South India, asks me how I acquired it. The senior Prabhus—she was fourteen when they married—are the grandparents of my student, Shoba Devi Pilar. The class assignment, I explain, required students to locate photos of female relatives, identify them, and provide some details about their situation and experiences. Shoba was surprised to learn that her grandmother had died first, at age seventy-eight, while her grandfather lived to be ninety.

After the Indian departs, I watch three Spanish-speaking women examining the Latinas in the "Generations" collection. Victoria Andino Rios, a New York Puerto Rican in her thirties (1951), is both sexy and elegant, they agree. Was her husband up to the challenge, they wonder? Did he show her off—or mistreat her?

"Which section of UNESCO are you with?" a tall, distinguished-looking African man inquires. He identifies himself as a press attaché with the Somalian Mission. I explain that I teach Women's Studies at a college in New Jersey, and that I've brought this collection of photos to Paris for UNESCO's celebration of International Women's Day. "From all over the world? How come?" he asks. Jersey City is like New York City, I say: a hub of immigration, even today, as Latinos, Middle Easterners, and Asians fly into Newark Airport or taxi through the Holland Tunnel. The new arrivals move into a low-cost, urban community with a large African American population. Like the Irish, Italians, Germans, and Poles before them, they establish churches and mosques, publish their own newspapers, open grocery stores, beauty salons, and restaurants, too.

I don't often get a chance to boast about my college. It's not a university, after all. Just an open admissions institution for working-class students, many with weak skills, English as a second language, and little money. "Cinderella of the Jerseys," I sometimes call it. I smile now, as the legend *Jersey City State College* flashes on UNESCO's video display screens—not just in Main Hall but all over the complex.

Finally, at 5:00 p.m., we've got the walls covered. Just in time. A crowd has gathered, and young men in white jackets have begun passing around red and white wine along with cheese, pâté, and crackers. Some two hundred guests of the U.S. Mission mill around. Many seem mesmerized by the images; a few, standing very close to the walls, are reading the narratives.

A WOMAN INTRODUCES HERSELF AS DAFNA, an Israeli and a friend of a U.S. staff member. She's a middle school teacher, she says, with students from as many countries as mine. Perhaps she could do such a project with her kids: collect photos and family stories, and then make an exhibit. Could I tell her what we did in our classrooms? Of course. Our instructions to students have been used in many U.S. colleges. I tell Daphna that some Israelis saw *Generations* in December 1981 at the University of Haifa. My collaborator Barbara Rubin and I were there for the First International Interdisciplinary Congress on Women. Among three hundred scholars in attendance from thirty different countries, many took home our how-to handouts. In fact, while in Haifa, Barbara and I gave a talk to a group of high school history students on the pleasures and perils of studying one's own family. In the U.S., we said, peasants and shopkeepers often became factory workers and maids. Our students heard tales of poverty, frustration, sacrifice, and struggle. Sometimes they uncovered secrets, and the secrets produced tears.

When *Generations of Women: In Search of Female Forebears* first opened at Jersey City State College in April 1980, we never imagined the travels to come. However, within a few months, we were showing the photos at feminist events, scholarly meetings, college art galleries, local libraries, and regional museums. Among my favorite sites, I say, was a gallery in a mall where shoppers on their way to Bloomingdale's or Saks couldn't help seeing the images. Some even ventured in.

A TRAVELING EXHIBIT, AND THIS ONE is no exception, relies on connections. Mary Ann Whitten and I became close friends during my Fulbright year in Tunisia. Her husband Ben was on the U.S. Embassy's cultural staff, as librarian. Mary-Ann, also a trained librarian, worked as a consultant to the English Department of the University of Tunis. Mary Ann, Ben, my late husband Eli, and I enjoyed a happy connection to wine (both Tunisian red and French), freshly baked baguettes, and socializing in Franco-American circles. After Tunisia, we stayed in touch. When the Whittens visited us in Leonia in the summer of 1982, I covered the bedside tables of the guest room with articles about *Generations of Women* and small glossies of the big images. I sold the show to Mary Ann, and she sold it to her (female) boss at UNESCO, Ambassador Jean Girard. Ambassador Girard subsequently wrote a glowing letter about *Generations,* which helped us place the show at the United Nations in August 1983.

FROM PARIS, I TAKE *GENERATIONS* TO DUBLIN—not the actual photos, which are promised for another week to UNESCO, but slides. My friend Ron Clifton, Public Affairs Officer at the U.S. Embassy in Dublin, held a similar position with the embassy in Tunis during that Fulbright year. When Ron learned that I would be in Paris with the exhibit for International Women's Day, he offered to add Dublin to my itinerary. Would I come to Ireland, he asked, for the week of March 13 to lecture on *Generations* and meet with Irish feminists?

The U.S. Embassy in Dublin is a round, fortress-like building. Thirty invited guests, all women, line up outside the Embassy to be checked for weapons by an electronic screening device and U.S. Marines. Inside, in the Embassy's central rotunda, the atmosphere is warm and convivial. An Embassy bartender mixes drinks to order (I restrict myself to white wine) while members of the Women's Political Association and the Irish Countrywomen's Association introduce themselves to me. What a delight, the Countrywomen's president says, that the Embassy has seen fit to put on a women's program.

Once the preliminaries are over, I launch into the slide talk. Katherine Keogh, my first photo (Irish-American, of course) offers a classic immigrant woman's tale. Born in 1850 and raised in a convent outside Dublin, she learned from the nuns "to speak English without a brogue." She also learned needlework, which allowed her, as an Irish immigrant, to avoid domestic service. Katherine traveled to the U.S. alone at age sixteen, I report. She was fortunate in being able to join her two sisters, who had recently settled in Brooklyn. After marrying an Irishman, a shipwright, she bore five children.

Her life, as filtered through several generations of family stories, was a continuous struggle for dignity and a decent living.

The audience is intrigued by the familiar threads of Katherine Keogh's story and her dignified appearance. They note the images of other poor immigrant women and African American women who seem almost regal in dress, posture, and setting. Often, I say, it's the magic of studio portraits: the subject captured in her best clothes, seated on an elegant chair, in front of a velvet curtain. Looking straight at the photographer, the Katherine Keoghs in our collection appear composed and at home in the world.

The Irish women who have been looking at my slides know this phenomenon; surely, they have their own grandmothers and great-grandmothers framed on their dressers and side tables. They know how photographs mask reality and allow us all to dream.

Dreams travel well, as visitors to *Generations of Women* always remark. Dreams make good press copy for an edgy feminist exhibit. Yes, give us the bitter truths of women's lives; but give us the illusions that helped these women make it through—and help us, too.

POST CARD: TENNIS COURT
CONNECTION, MOZAMBIQUE, 1993

W*ITH TIME TO KILL IN MAPUTO—and the streets less than safe for an unaccompanied American woman—I sign up for tennis lessons with Paolo, the pro at my hotel. He has an elegant slice backhand and clearly enunciated Portuguese. On the court, I forget my frustrations with the Mozambican professor in charge of my consultation and concentrate on bending my knees as I attack the ball.*

When the lesson ends, I grab a seat in the shade next to an animated, dark-haired woman in a crisp tennis dress. "I'm Ellie," she says before asking, in English, what brings me to Mozambique. I'm an academic, I explain, working on improving teaching about the United States at the Pedagogic Institute. "Oh, you must meet my husband," she responds. "Can you come for dinner tomorrow night?"

I haven't lacked for good food in Maputo. The restaurant at the Hotel Polana may be the best in the country. But I am hungry for conversation and weary of CNN for company. Ellie's invitation delights me. As we kiss goodbye, she says, "You'll enjoy talking with my husband. He's the American ambassador."

I do enjoy him—along with some excellent Portuguese white wine.

For a half-hour, we chat about Brazil, his first posting, where he met his wife. Then he's called to the phone. He's in the middle of negotiations, an aide reports, between the leftist Frelimo and the governing Renamo to end Mozambique's raging civil war. In fact, a peace accord was signed a year ago in Rome. But that hasn't stopped the killings or made the streets safe. Can Ambassador Friedman make a difference? How much money is the U.S. offering? Is this a case study for the Pedagogic Institute?

GUINEA: LESSONS
FROM THE FIELD, 1998

Arrival: 10 October 1998

The humidity clings to my tee shirt as I enter the Conakry Airport. The outside temperature is pressing toward three figures. Inside, air conditioning creates a familiar chill, but almost everything else is strange. I follow my U.S. colleague Jeanette, an experienced Guinea hand, through unmarked stations for passport control, visa control, and disease control. The government of Guinea requires proof of yellow fever inoculations. "*Ici,*" I say to a suspicious Guinean official, pointing to the bottom line on my yellow health card where the inoculation is indicated—in English, which he cannot read. I marvel that a country with the worst health care in the world is so exigent about protecting its visitors from yellow fever—or its citizens from contamination by visitors.

The final hurdle before leaving the airport is luggage control. Ahead of Jeanette now, I approach a portly policewoman who is spitting pumpkin-seed shells onto the ground all around her. "*Bon-*

jour," I say as I hand her my passport.

"*Vous avez un cadeau pour moi?*" she responds, opening her right hand. She wants a gift from me? What gift? When I feign ignorance, she repeats what is clearly not a request but a demand. I turn to Jeanette, who proffers a 5,000 Guinea franc note (about five U.S. dollars). The policewoman scowls and waves us through.

Outside, Jeanette scans the crowd for our colleague from CELA (The Center for the Study of the English Language) at the University of Conakry. I scan it too, dazzled by the local dress in brilliant hues and wild patterns set against a dung-colored landscape. Barely two minutes later, a stocky man in a gray safari-style suit greets me with an ebullient, "Welcome to Conakry!"

I turn my back, certain that he's a cabdriver ready to run a scam on me. But no. It's Diarra, the administrator of our faculty development project. A gracious man, he appears not to have taken offense at my rudeness. Doubtless he's accustomed to the confusion, or should I say the paranoia, of American visitors confronting so different a world.

Driving around Conakry in CELA's rusted out van, I look for the telltale signs of a capital city: hotels flanked by doormen in livery, high-end shops, well-tended plazas and parks. Instead I see miles of tar-paper shacks with tin roofs held in place by old rubber tires. I see pitted roads with open sewers and traffic lights that do not function. I see women loaded down with food, children, and laundry, while men sit around playing cards or dozing.

CELA: The Center for the Study of the English Language

We pull into a dusty yard with a single palm tree, a satellite dish, and a pair of colorless, one-story cinderblock buildings. There is no sign identifying the site, only a weathered bulletin board with a tacked-on list of English classes. In a few days, when the semester begins, the eight classrooms, library, and conference room will be filled to beyond capacity. English, it seems, is on the verge of breaking the francophone barrier. For the fall of 1998, a hundred new students have registered for the degree program, seventy more than the department's budget and scheduled classes can accommodate. "We don't have enough chairs," Diarra laments.

Supported by a grant from USAID, which Jeanette administers through the University of Delaware, CELA addresses Guinea's isolation from the Anglophone West. Students learning English should be able to participate in global aspects of national development. In a country where books, newspapers, and media resources are in desperately short supply, CELA faculty and students have access to a television and videotapes, along with an English-language library and computers. I note that the television is wedged into a space that allows for only three viewers at a time. Two computers, the Center's lifeline to the outer world, are frequently down due to power outages or the lack of technical support. Shrouded in plastic against the dust and the damp, they telegraph dysfunction. The library, with a miscellaneous collection of books in English, is run by a librarian who does not speak English.

The thirteen men and one woman in my seminar, three with the surname Diallo, are English language teachers and teacher trainers. Some have only a B.A., and none has a Ph.D. They are paid a paltry two hundred U.S. dollars a month, often supporting extended families of fifteen to twenty people. Although most work second jobs (as tutors and translators), they seem energetic and upbeat. I am energetic and upbeat, too. And why not? I'm getting paid to visit a little-known and troubled corner of West Africa thanks largely to my conversational French and familiarity with teaching conditions in very poor Third World universities.

The topic for our first session is family-centered oral history as pedagogy. In Guinea, where illiteracy runs around seventy-five percent, oral history is pedagogy with a purpose: a means of creating a cultural and historical record. Equally important, oral history is an effective strategy for developing communication skills—in listening, interviewing, analyzing data, translating, and reporting to a group. When this topic was proposed some months ago, I knew nothing about the politics of oral history in Guinea. It seems that Sekou Touré, the celebrated father of Guinean independence—and the African anti-colonial struggle—who became one of Africa's most infamous dictators, first embraced and then attacked the oral tradition. A Marxist, he considered it a reactionary practice, fostering tribalism at the expense of the nation-state.

Fifteen years after Touré's death, ethnicity remains a powerful force in Guinea, as it is in so much of the world. CELA faculty members are attached to their tribal roots. Indeed, the oral tradition resonates for them as a repository of cherished cultural values. But what is the place of undergraduate-level English in an oral history project in multi-ethnic, multi-lingual Guinea—where interviews must be conducted in Fula, Malinke, and Susu, the dominant tribal languages? If the interviews are to become part of a national "record," wouldn't it be more useful to translate them into French rather than English?

Language isn't the only barrier to transferring this pedagogy from the U.S. to Guinea. Family-centered oral history—as I use it in teaching—is research with a therapeutic dimension. The interview is an opportunity for a life review. I warn student interviewers that getting the story from a parent or grandparent may require invading their subjects' privacy and then absorbing their anger or tears.

How do these psychological preoccupations play in a traditional, clan-centered culture? In a realm where rituals of address and hierarchies of authority regulate who talks to whom about what subjects? Where honor and shame can be more powerful than empathy? Not well, to judge from the reactions around the table. Nevertheless, several seminar participants begin to envision students interviewing family members—to develop an anatomy of village relationships and survival strategies. At the end of our two-and-a-half-hour session, the Guineans have transformed this distinctly American pedagogy into a project on the dynamics of ethnic group life. It's been a tough morning's work, and I'm ready for a shower before lunch.

And a swim. Our hotel, the Camayenne, easily passes for Paradise in Conakry. The handsome pool has its own bar and open-air restaurant. For an hour each afternoon, I place my well-oiled body on a comfortable chaise next to the well-oiled bodies of a half-dozen (white) Sabena Airline crew members. With no additional effort, the "real Conakry" disappears from sight.

Two days later, I launch the second seminar entitled "What Is American Studies?" I begin, conventionally enough, by speaking about interdisciplinarity and multiculturalism in American studies;

about the tension between diverse interests and cultures, on the one hand, and the unifying force of law, technology, and popular culture on the other. When my audience appears impatient with this professional discourse, I speak more concretely: suggesting ways in which African Americans since the Civil Rights Movement have altered the American landscape. I mention marches, strikes, and the legacy of Martin Luther King.

My comments on Black empowerment open Pandora's Box. Suddenly, Guineans are attacking African Americans—for drug abuse, crime, single parenthood, and welfare dependency; for squandering their opportunities and failing to achieve. The subtext of this attack is the superiority of traditional Guinean values: Muslim faith, duty to family and clan, hard work, and delayed gratification—values, I hear CELA faculty asserting, that would stand them and their children in good stead in America.

I jump into the fray, reminding my audience of pervasive racism in the U.S., as well as increasing ghettoization, negative media representations, and the loss of jobs in the post-industrial economy as reasons for despair among American Blacks. My interventions fall on mostly deaf ears. The seminar is divided, with the loudest voices attacking African Americans for displaying American behaviors (violence, loss of respect for authority, and social disorganization), which seminar members find offensive. I wonder: Are these qualities and behaviors that *they* personally fear as urbanization erodes tribal norms in Guinea? Are the behaviors of marginalized American Blacks an affront to them as Africans because they are almost certain to be taken for African-Americans when they visit the U.S.?

Leaving: 18 October 1998

The Camayenne's gift shop, with a striking display of local crafts, allows guests to bring home souvenirs while avoiding the city's open sewers, aggressive beggars, and enervating humidity. I buy several expensive mono-prints made by Diarra's wife, which I mention to our host while sending my compliments to the artist. I select a few small silver pieces and consider but reject two striking bread baskets in natural tones. My suitcase and carry-on have their limits.

Waiting in the lobby for Diarra to escort us to the airport, Jeanette and I say goodbye to Marie Jose, a Belgian businesswoman. One of the principal exporters of steel to Guinea, Marie Jose bonded with us three days earlier over white wine and chicken salad. In a confidential tone, she complained that in this country nobody knows how to work and nothing works, including the banks. The banks, she fumed, will not change local money into hard currency—she does this on the street—and will not transfer funds abroad. How do you get money out of the country, we asked? That's when we learned about Mahmoud, the dapper chief of police with whom we noticed her dining the previous evening. He's a simple man, she said, her precise Belgian French full of scorn—simple but necessary to Marie Jose's enterprise. When she flies home to Brussels, she carries her profits in her pocketbook—in cash. What if they open your bag at the airport? Jeanette asked? That's where Mahmoud comes in, she said.

Indeed. In less than two hours, we'll observe the chief of police—with Marie Jose's embroidered handbag on his shoulder—escorting his Belgian patron through Customs and onto her plane.

AT THE AIR FRANCE COUNTER, an officious attendant insists that my overstuffed carry-on must be checked in. Checked in? This bag has no locks. For a split second, I wonder if a little *cadeau* to the Air France guy would make a difference. Turning to Diarra, a savvy man but no Mahmoud, I point to my four unprotected zipper compartments. My gesture reads like a loudspeaker announcement. Immediately two young lock vendors appear, thrusting similar sets of small locks in our direction. Each insists that he got there first and the deal is his. They jog forward and sideways, touching our arms and our shoulders, beseeching us with their needs and their young children's needs. "Where's the justice?" the shorter guy wails. Jeanette and I pull back, frightened by this escalation of hostilities. Diarra, sweating profusely, takes a step toward the wailer, hands him 2,000 Guinea francs and collects the locks. Heart racing, I secure my suitcase, check in and walk rapidly toward the departure lounge.

Amadou Diallo: An Immigrant from Guinea in New York

On 4 February 1999—about a month after I wrote the preceding paragraphs—Amadou Diallo, a twenty-two-year-old Guinean immigrant, was shot to death by four New York City police officers. The offending cops, all white and members of a special plainclothes Street Crime unit, fired a total of forty-one bullets at the young foreigner as he stood in the vestibule of his apartment house. Diallo was unarmed. The brutal shooting, with its associations to the Abner Louima case and other racially biased acts of police aggression, galvanized the African American community. The Reverend Al Sharpton brought Diallo's parents to New York from West

Africa, and organized press conferences and demonstrations. Black community leaders—along with clergy, civil libertarians, and civil rights activists—spoke out passionately against police brutality and the systemic harassment of minorities.

Sharpton's campaign of civil disobedience led to the arrest of some 1,200 individuals—including religious leaders of many faiths, Hollywood personalities, and former Mayor David Dinkins. Activists, denouncing aggressive, "no tolerance" policing, called attention to the negative impact of Mayor Rudy Giuliani's Quality of Life Campaign on communities of color.

The Diallo story received extensive media coverage. Featured on page one of the *New York Times*—for two weeks after the shooting—were accounts of the young street peddler's clean-living habits, his middle-class family's history in and out of Guinea, and the travails of West African immigrants in the city. The day Diallo was buried in Hollande Bouru, a village founded by his grandfather that still lacks running water and electricity, the *Times* printed a map of West Africa showing Guinea on the westernmost edge and the city of Conakry protruding into the Atlantic.

Before Diallo there was hardly a person in my circle who could locate Guinea on a map of the world. Several well-traveled friends confused the small francophone country with New Guinea in the South Pacific and French Guiana on the northern rim of South America. The exception was an African American painter and passionate pan-Africanist who had visited the country in the mid '70's. "You'll just love Conakry," Ben promised me. "It's a simple, unspoiled African place, not built up and not Europeanized."

Lessons From The Field

I think about the Diallos in my seminar—and all those Guineans who share a name as common there as Jones or Lee in America; I think about the would-be immigrants from Guinea, prompted by this recent racial nightmare to re-consider their dream of Opportunity in America. How fortunate I was to lecture at CELA before Diallo, when I passed as a (somewhat) innocent White woman—an academic tourist in a Third World country provoking a pleasant exchange with African colleagues.

But after Diallo? After Diallo, my program might well have been canceled. At best, I would have been an unwelcome American Studies specialist: someone not trusted to report fairly about the situation of American Blacks or the significance of the Civil Rights Movement. The murder of Amadou Diallo and thousands of innocent people of color by White Americans is a story that Black Africans know in their bones: from their own experience of colonialism. They know these power inequities better than I ever will.

WE ARE ALL NARROWLY CENTERED, especially when we leave behind the comforts and familiarity of home. When we travel, we push outward, testing ourselves and our capacity for openness. Can we read the signs? Make sense of the language and the body language? Decipher the code of politesse? Find locals who will help us understand where we are? The other side of curiosity is fear and confusion. My painter friend Ben tried to warn me not to look for the First World in the Third. Appreciating difference is demanding work, he should have said, requiring more than good intentions.

As my trip to Guinea makes clear, understanding often begins with confusion. Understanding requires not just time and distance but also the discomfort of self-criticism. Understanding, I believe, can emerge from writing. And re-writing. And from returning to what's been written. . .as I do here, after almost twenty years.

POST CARD: THE HILLS DON'T HAVE EARS, CZECH REPUBLIC, 1993–94

*T*HE GRAND FACADE OF PILSEN'S HOTEL CONTINENTAL, *built in 1895, doesn't prepare me for the run-down lobby or un-smiling service. Is this the heritage of Communism? I ask myself. It's the Fall of 1993, four years after the breakup of the Soviet Union; I'm visiting the Czech Republic to "promote" American Studies at the University of West Bohemia.*

For two busy weeks, I meet with colleagues, students, and administrators. In this new era for their nation, they want me to know, the U.S. is The Land of Opportunity and English is everyone's foreign language of choice. American Studies will succeed at their university.

My knowledge of the Czech Republic begins and ends with glowing reports about Vaclav Havel's Velvet Revolution—separating (the former) Czechoslovakia from the Soviet Union without waging war. Correction: as a New Yorker, I've sought out Czech duck at Vasata, a gracious East Side "destination," and I sometimes order Pilsen beer. Now, in the hotel's restaurant, I mention my passion for duck to the host. "Finally," he says, "after decades of being forced to adhere to dull Soviet recipes—stipulated amounts of meat, fat, flour, and milk—we can recover our own Czech cuisine."

As planned, I return six months later for another two weeks of convivial talks. My schedule concludes with a gathering at the country house of the University Rector. Dr. H. is eager to show off his terrain to foreign guests—especially the surrounding hills. We climb, following a narrow path, for about an hour. "During Communism," he explains, "these hills were my refuge. I'd come with one trusted friend. Here we could speak truly. The hills don't have ears."

RALPH LAUREN'S YURT, CHINA, 1999

A T HEAVENLY LAKE, 6,500 FEET above sea level, in the midst of the Tian Shan (heavenly) Mountains, seven middle-aged American women marvel at China's alpine wonderland. We've traveled sixty miles from Urumqi, a Central Asian city mired in pollution. Now, near the water's edge, we pause at stalls where Kazakh merchants have laid out brown, phallic-looking roots and mushrooms in the shape of lunar sculptures. His and hers. Yin and yang. I picture the erotic objects on my coffee table and the wry comments they will elicit. "Competition for Eli's plays on porn," someone is sure to say. Yes and no. Chinese medicine for healthy living, our Chinese guide Carl explains. Should we stock up? They've got to be cheaper than the Chinese-based dietary supplements sold in American health food stores for arthritic joints, balky knees, and flagging energy.

Our group piles into a small ferry boat with a dozen Chinese tourists. Three of the Chinese are wedded to their cell phones. The rest take their ritualistic turn, standing before the group, alone and in pairs, to be photographed by all their compatriots. I am traveling without a camera, leaving this kind of documentation to the postcard industry—and to my picture-taking companions whose set-ups, unlike those of the Chinese, are generally self-mocking. Of course, the postcards I write and collect have the same function as both types of photographs: to possess the journey, in my fashion; and to prove to those back home that I had the wit—and the means—to make it.

"This is the Switzerland of China," Carl proclaims, "and the Queen of Heaven is in residence." I sense her presence in the purified atmosphere—in the crisp, clean air that fills my lungs. I feel unexpectedly calm. I also feel in possession of myself—a rare sensation on a tightly scheduled packaged tour crammed with history, culture, and commercial distractions. Staying focused, decoding, and remembering all require more effort than I'm willing to acknowledge.

Suddenly, the boat turns toward the shore. Twelve blissful, meditative minutes from start to finish, and we're back on land.

Our bus negotiates the slopes of the Tian Shan Mountains, where Kazakh herders tend their sheep and goats. There are no villages here, only yurts: round, tent-like structures with slightly flattened conical roofs that provide shelter for the nomads and their families.

We park in front of a large, gussied-up yurt with a life-size stuffed camel, blanketed and harnessed, gracing the front yard. Next to the camel sits a round red table, signaling that tea is served within. I wonder, did Carl ring up on his cell phone to announce our arrival and make a reservation for seven?

As we approach the yurt, an old woman and a small girl appear on the road. Immediately, my six traveling companions reach for their cameras. The woman and child, recognizing a business opportunity, stop immediately and face the photographers. They do not smile. After the clicking and flashing cease, the woman asks for three yuan (less than fifty American cents) from each of the six Americans. "Three yuan? Really?" The Americans are indignant. Does the old woman take them for fools? At Heavenly Lake, the going rate for elaborately staged photo-ops with horses and ethnic attire was two yuan apiece. Without discussion, my friends each hand the woman two yuan and turn quickly toward the yurt.

The doorway of the yurt is outlined with bright red, orange and yellow embroidery. Inside, wool carpets in bold floral patterns cover every inch of the dirt floor. Stacked along the walls are dozens of woven cushions in hues of deep red, purple, blue, and green. Two antique-looking white lace dresses and several colorful vests hang from a wire at the rear. It's a dazzling display, like an ad for Pottery Barn or Ralph Lauren's newest line of exurban attire.

A Kazakh woman with a worn, lined face ushers us in. We wonder: Is she the entrepreneurial owner, or the wife of the owner—or a tenant, or a government employee? She wears a threadbare cotton skirt and a dirty sweatshirt with the legend *Esprit* in big letters. I picture a grateful U.S. tourist giving her the sweatshirt after enjoying a cup of tea. But I immediately reject this construction as naive. The realities of late twentieth-century globalization and Chinese entrepreneurship suggest that the sweatshirt—not real Esprit but an Esprit knockoff—was made in China for local consumption as well as for export. Foreign labels like Esprit, Adidas, and Levi's have a cache wherever we've traveled in post-Maoist China.

Everything in the yurt is for sale, Carl informs us. While we absorb this commercial opportunity, our hostess prepares tea with mare's milk on an outside fire. Then, from her "real" house a few feet away, a small, dirty-looking yurt surrounded by rubble, she brings dried yogurt cheese, fried bread, and home-made candy. Do were dare eat the cheese? Is the bread "safer"? Or the candy? We sniff each of the items, taking the smallest possible bites. Refreshments, we understand, are a gesture of hospitality to the traveler and a come-on to the tourist-as-shopper. Indeed, encountering the rugs, pillows, and items of Kazakh clothing in something like their native setting is enticing. Or should be. When confronted by indigenous crafts, I habitually lose control of my credit card. A week ago, at the Friendship Store in Beijing, several of us loaded up on woven purses and pillow covers from other parts of Central Asia. But here nobody buys.

How come? Is the yurt-as-boutique an offense to our cultural sophistication? To our touristic, fantasy-driven innocence? Back home at the Bergen Mall, I would treasure a Central Asian boutique with the ambiance of a yurt: a shop designed as a quasi-museum to heighten the pleasure of as-if buying and vicarious travel. And so would my companions. But this postcard-perfect herder's house where nobody actually lives, in the midst of the Taklimakan Desert, violates our notions of Shop and Yurt. We have traveled more than three thousand miles west from Beijing to Xinjiang Province in search of some dream of China-before-globalization and before state-mandated homogenization—e.g., Minority Nationalities, as the guides refer to them—like the Kazakhs, in their seemingly unchanging and "authentic" habitat. We arrive only to be lured into an ersatz yurt while the real thing, only a stone's throw away, is protected from our prying eyes.

Looking back, I see that the items for sale in Ralph Lauren's yurt are window dressing. They disguise the government's real object, which is to sell tourism in Xinjiang Province. The sell is subtle and brilliant. Not the straightforward, aggressive, in-your-face Chinese manner we've become accustomed to, but an elaborate con job: an environment designed to satisfy our fantasies. We leave the yurt empty-handed, without paying for the refreshments. There's no need, Carl explains. The visit is a part of the tour, like the twelve-minute boat ride on Heavenly Lake, and the huge, modern, road-side gift shop—which welcomes credit cards, dollars, and yuan—where we will make our pit stop before returning to Urumqi.

Leaving the yurt, we spot the old woman, now on the other side of the road, motioning to the child, doubtless her granddaughter, to join her. The little girl has been freshly dressed in a pink-and-red frock. At her side is the family's pet goat, a long-haired creature with a glossy white coat and a red ribbon and tassels between its horns. Like an Upper East Side French poodle just back from the hairdresser. Apparently, grandma is hoping for another lucrative photo-op. But no. We've become impatient with staging. Besides, we are all remembering a fat-cheeked boy at Heavenly Lake with his impeccably groomed goat, both standing motionless for what seemed like an eternity. Stopping Time for us, the boy and his pet earned a living. While grandma and grandchild are doing their best, they're not in the same league.

POST CARD: LOTUS ENERGY, NEPAL, 1997

A LARGE MAP OF NEPAL OPPOSITE MY SON'S DESK *features a flower garden of push-pins: one for every hundred solar power units in some seventy-five towns and remote villages. Lotus Energy, the Kathmandu company Adam runs with another American ex-pat, was among the first solar businesses established in one of the world's most impoverished countries. "Nineteen million people live here," Adam tells me, "with a life expectancy of fifty-three years and a per capita income of $170.00. Ninety percent without electricity." Digesting these figures takes me some time; in truth, it might take a lifetime. How would I manage without a toilet or electric lights? Without a refrigerator, Kleenex, or a reliable dentist?*

The partners started Lotus Energy in 1992 with two notebook computers and very little cash. Among their invisible assets were fearlessness, idealism, and a good ear for Nepali, the dominant local language. Also, a heavy tolerance for dahl bhat *(lentils and rice), cows in the road, insane traffic patterns, and putrid air.*

In a short time, they were building solar power systems and installing them in sites often four hours on foot from the nearest bus stop. "I love seeing the excitement of villagers," Adam says, "when they get their first system. Kids can study after dark while adults work on their crafts. Families relax together watching sports on TV." Dreadful pollution provoked a related, major effort: bringing electric vehicles to Nepal.

Adam introduces me to Pete and Penny, student interns from Oregon. They've traveled more than seven thousand miles (on their own dollar) to learn how solar units work and to teach Nepali villagers to operate them. What an enviable education for twenty-year-old Americans—making change with Lotus Energy rather than reading about it, and getting credit, too!

WOMEN'S LIVES—STORIES FROM MY GUATEMALAN TEACHER, 2000–08

THREE MONTHS AFTER HER GRADUATION from high school, Susana tells me, her sister Olivia became pregnant. Many of her seventeen-year-old friends in Huehuetenango, Guatemala, already had their first babies. A few were expecting a second. Olivia—slender, fair, and born with a slight limp—had always felt "damaged" and at a disadvantage in the mating game. As a result, she had opted to marry down and "dark." At the church wedding, Susana continues, her mother had wept until she made herself ill. It wasn't just the pregnancy, but the new family on the doorstep: Olivia's drug-dealing husband, his brother in the business, and his sister selling sex.

It's January 2000. I listen to this distressing story my Guatemalan Spanish teacher, Susana, is telling me. Other people's distress is not boring. Our two weeks together, focused on conversation, should keep me riveted. Recently retired, I've come to Guatemala for a break from the New Jersey winter and also to improve my fluency. In Susana I've found a personable and skilled instructor. What's more, as a Women's Studies professor who spent years collecting other women's stories, I've stumbled upon a gifted informant—and a goldmine of material for a new, still-to-be-imagined writing project.

Susana's improvised *telenovela* is the dramatic center of our daily work. There is her own saga, with quick cuts to her mother's story and her sister's—as well as the doings of neighbors, friends, and former classmates. Like her sister, Susana became pregnant out of wedlock. But not until after she finished her degree in English. Her lover, Rodrigo, also a university graduate, was married and the father of two children. After seven years of living with Susana and their two kids, he is still not divorced. However, Rodrigo's marital status doesn't (usually) trouble my teacher—nor does it prevent her mother from adoring this son-in-law.

Sitting opposite Susana, I lean across the narrow table, our private carrel (and classroom) in the garden of el Centro de Lenguas. For two hours every morning, from 8:00 to 10:00 a.m., we exchange a mix of personal information, cultural commentary, and intimate anecdotes. Susana corrects my grammar without interrupting the flow. When I pause mid-sentence, she quickly produces the word I am fishing for.

Susana's first round of stories are a challenge. Nothing in my experience matches their deep-in-the-bone pain. Almost nothing. Reaching for my worst humiliation, I tell Susana about becoming pregnant with a (secretly) married lover. Of course, he refuses my pleas to marry (while never explaining why), but he willingly pays for my abortion. That was in 1962, I say, while I was finishing my graduate work.

While Susana would like abortion as an option, she can't imagine going this route. "In Guatemala, we have our babies," she says. Some women give them up, I know. I see American women here in the cafes every day, with their adopted babies—a shade or two darker than the new moms—wrapped snugly against their chests.

And after that cad? Susana asks. "I was careful. Very careful," I say. During my first college-teaching job, far away in the wilds of Vermont, I was attracted to two married colleagues—and scared I would do something stupid. When classes ended in May, I resigned and returned, without another job, to New York. "Four years later," I continue, "I got lucky." I describe the sexy painter and professor of art with whom I flirted in the faculty dining room at Queens College. "He left his wife for me," I confess, as Susana smiles knowingly.

JANUARY, 2002: I ALMOST FAIL TO RECOGNIZE Susana. On the patio opposite the office of el Centro de Lenguas, I see an olive-skinned woman, surrounded by a knot of female colleagues, holding forth. Susana's face is fuller; she's thirty pounds heavier than two years earlier and wearing glasses. But she hasn't lost her confident posture—shoulders thrust back—or the zest that seems built into her speech.

Once we've settled into our carrel-in-the-garden, we pick up the conversation where we left off two years ago. "What's new with Rodrigo?" I ask. Rodrigo is also an English teacher, at another language school, and he has a second job at a car-rental place.

"We're fine," she says. "He comes and goes as usual. Last night, for example, he returned late after having a beer with the guys. No, he doesn't call—that wouldn't be manly—but he wakes me to say he's home. '*Quieres algo?*' I always ask. Would you like something, perhaps some soup? 'No,' he'll say, 'I just want you to know I'm here.'"

To my astonishment, Susana reports that not being married to Rodrigo gives her more freedom than marriage would. Especially since she has her education, her job, and her salary. If they were married, Susana explains, she'd worry about the complications of a divorce if Rodrigo were to leave her. Or she might feel pressured to consult with him about purchases for the house or small matters involving the kids. If they were married, according to Guatemalan law, she couldn't take their children out of the country without his permission—while he is free to do so without checking with her.

Being married, most women know, does not guarantee fidelity or domestic harmony. Susana's father married her mother only after their third child, a boy, was born. So long as there were only girls, he saw no need to marry. Her father, she's quick to add, was a heavy drinker, often violent, and no bargain as a husband or lover. In one of his alcoholic fits, he hit her mother so hard in the pelvic area that she required emergency surgery.

The weight gain, Susanna tells me, is the result of hormone injections for birth control. She wants to have her tubes tied, but Guatemalan law requires that a woman younger than thirty must obtain her husband's written permission. Rodrigo isn't Susana's husband, and she's not yet thirty. Susana is counting the months—only five to go. "Will we ever get beyond these sexist arrangements?" she asks. I hear her anger and remain silent. What will it take to change the law in a Catholic and deeply sexist culture? How is it that we American women—with abundant education and resources—haven't managed more control over our bodies and our lives? We used to blame the Catholic Church; it was an easier target than husbands or other family men, easier than corporations, government, and institutional arrangements (including places of employment) that benefited from women's dependence.

"How are things with Olivia?" I ask.

After two children and steady abuse, Susana says, Olivia has returned with her daughter and son to her mother's tiny house. She still lives there, along with their much indulged twenty-eight-year-old brother, a university student. "My sister and brother are trying to push my mother out of her own house," Susana continues, "and they have put the property in their names." Her siblings want to be sure that Susana, who now has her own small place with Rodrigo, will not inherit a share of their mother's home.

So much drama! And pain! With two children scheming to control her estate, Susana's mother—a high school history teacher—is feeling the pressure. Recently, she offered to borrow money to help Susana and Rodrigo complete construction on their house. When the interior wall dividing the children's space from the parents' is finished, she proposes to move into the children's room with four-year-old Paula and two-year-old Vito. Oh, no! How humiliating for a fifty-year-old professional woman. And not the family arrangement that Susana and Rodrigo have in mind.

Meanwhile, Olivia remains involved with the family of her not-quite ex-husband, who continues to threaten her when he visits their children. On any given evening, Susana says, someone in the family is sure to be drunk, drugging or dealing. The husband's sister, the brothel owner, carries a sharpened knife in her apron. The brother-in-law, a long-distance trucker, supplies "fresh blood" to the sister's "house"—girls often as young as thirteen. Since virgins bring the highest price in the sex trade, the traffic in very young women is especially lucrative.

This *trafico sexual*, Susana reports, grows out of the family's history. The ex-husband's mother was sold into prostitution at age fourteen to help pay the family's bills, and so was the sister who now makes a living from the trade. It's normal, Susana says, for girls from very poor families to be exploited in this fashion. And then to exploit others.

I ask what keeps Olivia in this world she claims to despise. Habit, self-hatred, or some strange fascination with violence? Susana doesn't know. She says Olivia doesn't know either.

SHE WAS IN A MATERNITY CLINIC, waiting to see her gynecologist, Susana reports, plunging into her newest tale. Sitting beside her in the waiting room was a girl with a mark on her left cheek in the shape of a shoe. "What happened to you?" Susana asked. To help expel her baby, a midwife sat on top of her, the girl explained, and pressed down on the womb. When the midwife's pressures failed to liberate the baby, the young woman's mother-in-law hit her with a shoe and pronounced her "good for nothing." The baby died in the hospital a few hours later.

Women, Susana says, are often brutal to one another. Is the violence exercised by men their model? I wonder. How would my feminist colleagues back home respond? It's commonplace to celebrate women's "difference"—our superiority to men in grasping the human consequences of particular economic and power relations; also, our "instinct," dare I say, for putting the needs of individuals first. I'm generally in the camp of women's difference. But unlike Susana, I've seen few instances of women dishing out physical abuse.

JANUARY 2004: "HOW ARE THINGS WITH RODRIGO," I ask as Susana and I settle into our familiar seats. What I mean but don't say is, *Any news about marriage?* I'm laughing hard as I unwrap the question for Susana. In the late '60s, when Eli and I were living together before we married, my mother would begin every telephone call to me with "How are things," her code for *Any action on your marriage?* In those years, in our middle-class Jewish New York circles, we knew no unmarried couples who lived together. My mother, a very conventional woman, loved Eli but did not appreciate our outlaw status.

"Rodrigo would be happy to be divorced," Susana tells me. *But.* There's an inheritance he's been promised by an aged grandfather. Rodrigo fears that the old guy might change his mind if he divorced his wife, Elena—even though he has been living publicly with Susana for more than seven years. About a year ago, Elena's boyfriend came to Rodrigo, saying he wanted to marry her. Would Rodrigo give her a divorce? Fine, Rodrigo said. Let her initiate the proceedings. Elena, it turns out, is also interested in the promised inheritance; she's hanging on to her legal status. When she made this clear to the boyfriend, he took off. Elena is now alone and as bitchy as ever.

Susana rolls with these twists of fate. Is her secret natural savvy? Or hard-earned wisdom? Are the two the same? The notion of an easy ride doesn't enter her calculations; she seems free of material lusts and status ambitions. However, Susana is fiercely devoted to her teaching career and her personal development. Her students enlarge her world, she insists.

MAY 2011, LEONIA, NEW JERSEY: I RECEIVE AN EMAIL from Susana, the first ever, using her mother's email address. *They've fired me*, she writes. *I'm too depressed to say more.* What could have happened? Susana was among the school's top teachers: skilled with students at all levels; upbeat, personable, and reliable; valued by other staff members and the administration. Former students requested her, as I always did when pre-paying my fees. Over the years, I've recommended her to many friends. "You'll really enjoy Susana," I say. "Not only does she listen well and tell great stories about life in Guatemala—she explains strange idioms clearly and makes grammar seem simple."

I write to the director of the school, expressing my dismay. *Susana exploded at a student*, he responds almost immediately, *during an off-campus lesson. She was inappropriate, like a crazy woman.* A week later, I phone the Director in Guatemala. "It's a sad story," he says. "Her best friend on staff tells me that Rodrigo has left Susana for a young American student. She saw him on the street the day of the episode. We're all so sorry about this," he says.

POST CARD: THE DOCUMENTATION CENTER, GERMANY, 2016

W*E WALK THROUGH A SERIES OF DARK CORRIDORS, be-tween black-brick walls covered with photos, video screens, and print commentary in German and English. Sound assaults us: the shrill, impassioned speeches of the Führer; the marching feet of Nazi Party members; and the drum rolls and brass of military bands. We see the people of Nuremberg, smiling, cheering and saluting—swept away by the Party's message: Make Germany Great Again!*

On one screen, I watch a couple in their eighties being interviewed. They speak—nervously but clearly—about what they didn't know, how they went along, and why they were caught up in the political tide, wanting a better future for their families and their country. It's probably not the first time (or the last) that they have confronted (so bravely) their passivity and cowardice. They make this extraordinary effort, I feel, for their grandchildren, for future generations of Germans, and for people untested by fascism—who need to know. Their shame and their decency are palpable. I stand silently, uncomfortable in the face of these confessions. How would I have acted under similar circumstances? What is the lesson for democratic nations in the twenty-first century? The exhibit is titled Fascination and Terror. *I would have called it* Seduction and Terror.

The Documentation Center, Nuremberg's remarkable museum, sits famously on the Nazi Party rally grounds. While the term "Documentation Center" suggests floor-to-ceiling racks of file boxes, what we find instead is an emotionally shattering exhibit—evoking the allure of the Party's assertions of power and related evil machinations. The modern German nation, to its great credit, takes responsibility for the murder of six million Jews and others—and for Hitler's system of terror.

PATZCUARO DIARY, MEXICO, 2000

Plaza Grande, Plaza Chica

At 8:00 a.m., from my bench on the Plaza Grande, I watch the sweepers, the shoeshine man, the runners, the dog walker, and a stream of people on their way to work. In the middle of the Plaza stands a statue of Don Vasco de Quiroga, the Spanish priest who taught crafts to the local Purepecha people. To this day, copper, ceramics, weaving, and straw sculpture provide employment for artisans, shop owners, and even a few international shippers.

I've fled from the anxiety of the Bush–Gore election countdown, south of the border to Mexico's Western Highlands. In Patzcuaro, a handsome city of 60,000 where I've come to write, I relish the distractions—especially on its two principle plazas.

Shortly before 9:00 a.m., four young men fill plastic buckets with water from a fountain opposite Don Vasco and move to the perimeter. Soon enough, dirt-splattered trucks and a few filthy cars line up, ready for their morning bath. Campesinos in straw hats lounge in the shade; a pair of old women dressed in dark-blue-and-black-striped Purepecha *rebozos* rush past me, carrying fresh rolls in plastic sacks. Townspeople and villagers, Mexican tourists and foreigners—including Americans from *el Norte*—mix and blend with ease. Or so it appears. Nobody asks me if I can spare a few pesos, *por favor*.

About forty feet away, a young guy washes a stone bench. He soaps it with a rag and then scrubs it with a stiff, long-handled brush. Sixteen similar benches face inward on each side of the Plaza, a total of sixty-four. Is this a town project? I wonder. Are these beautifully crafted benches, with their curved backs and sculpted arms, all scheduled for a seasonal cleaning? A middle-aged man, in a white shirt and a gray wool pullover, shouts instructions to the worker. Is he urging more speed or more care? When the boss glances my way, I smile and approach him. Immediately, he introduces himself as Antonio. *Es un proyecto del pueblo?* (Is this a project of the town?), I ask.

The locals, I later learn, have heard Antonio's response hundreds of times. "These benches are mine," he tells me, "opposite my restaurant, a business I inherited from my father." He points across the street to a modest café and above it to the home that has been in his family for generations. Like many men in Patzcuaro, Antonio has spent time north of the border and enjoys chatting with people like me. "I was there five years, mostly in LA, driving a cab. In the States, it's not hard to make money," he says. But he prefers being here, living in the house in which he was born, looking out on the beautiful Plaza Grande.

Almost an hour has passed. I take my walk around the square before heading toward the nearby Plaza Chica. Less gracious than the Grande, the Plaza Chica is a hub for vendors selling flowers (marigolds during this fall season), clothing, housewares, jewelry, trinkets, newspapers, and magazines. The Chica leads into the Central Market, where I'm drawn by the smell of hot chicken soup. I see crowds of people eating *bocadillas*, small tortillas filled with roast pork, salsa, and cheese. The soup smells better than it looks, and the *bocadillas* look irresistible.

After several punishing experiences with Mexican street food, abstinence is now my rule: Montezuma may take his revenge on me, but not because I've issued an invitation. Leaving the Plaza Chica, I stop at the local *panederia* (bakery). The aromas of butter, sugar, chocolate, and cinnamon make me giddy with desire. I grab an aluminum tray and a pair of tongs, circle the open bins, and select two plain rolls, two apricot pastries, and an oversized raisin cookie. The cost is about $.50 American.

My morning walk around the two plazas is as invigorating as an hour of tennis, and less tiring. I marvel at the blue sky, bright sun, and clean dry air—along with the entertainment provided by street life. How fortunate I am to be in such an enticing and unfamiliar place—with a project of my own choosing, open to the pleasures of the moment.

Casa Don Miguel

Casa Don Miguel, where I am lodging for three weeks, is an oasis of calm. Its four inner gardens, I'm hoping, will help me cultivate at least one of my own. A friend who knew I was looking for a writer's retreat spotted this one, sponsored by a small arts foundation in Massachusetts. I sent them a few paragraphs about wanting to experience everyday life, using my Spanish, in a friendly Mexican city; and they sent me an invitation.

Day after day, I enjoy two tasty meals, a well-stocked library, and museum-quality handwoven rugs, masks, and pottery—all from the region. The rooms at the Casa are welcoming but chilly—except at midday (we're at 7,200 feet, somewhat higher than Denver). I have the luxury of a small electric heater in my room; it's the only one in the house. While the other guest rooms, the dining room, and library all have fireplaces, I'm grateful to be spared fussing with the fire.

Esperanza, the cook, arrives at 9:00 a.m. and makes coffee. Breakfast, scheduled for 10:00, is served at a round table on the patio in strong sunlight. I'm always happy with yogurt and fruit in the morning. However, Esperanza expects to cook for the Casa's guests (I'm the only one at the moment)—a cheese omelet this morning with warm sweet rolls and jam. The eggs arrive fluffy, the coffee strong and aromatic. No flies buzz around; no ants invade the jam. What more could I hope for?

After breakfast I return to my room and my laptop. Sitting on a hard chair with my back to the patio, I fret. "Encounters in Patzcuaro," my proposal declares, will track the experiences of a recently retired college professor and (reasonably fluent) Spanish speaker over three weeks in a tourist-friendly Mexican city. How does she spend her time? What puzzles or surprises her? What challenges does she seek out? And most critically: what does she learn about the place, the people, and herself? Here's the rub: In order to write, I must be out and doing.

I must also return to the Casa for *comida,* the midday meal, served at 2:00 p.m. Esperanza asks each morning what I would like: chicken, beef, fish, perhaps a baked pasta? For *comida* I sit with Brian, a twenty-something poet and the Casa's liaison with visiting artists, at a large square table in full sunlight. Brian wears a hat. I probably should buy one. Today's menu is creamed broccoli soup followed by a white fish in a garlicky cream sauce. Too much cream all around, but the tastes are fresh and clean. Only a fool would fuss.

Local Voices, Local Vistas

At 8:00 p.m., needing a margarita to cushion my (U.S.) Election forebodings, I head for El Patio, a cozy place on the Plaza Grande. I have with me the November 3 issue of *The New Yorker*, featuring Joe Klein's article on Gore's mistakes during the campaign. He squandered his opportunities, Klein writes, by heeding the dictates of consultants who kept changing their instructions. I underline a few key sentences while waiting for the oversized margarita to kick in.

Behind me, an English-speaking pair are talking about Casa de las Culturas, a museum of pre-Hispanic culture. It's not the museum that catches my attention so much as the New York accent of the woman and the cultured English of her companion. I renew my attack on the margarita and begin to feel buzzed. Smiling, I turn to the couple behind me, apologize for interrupting their conversation, and begin moaning about Bush's likely win. I'm in luck. The woman is a painter living on the Democratic Upper West Side of Manhattan, my neighborhood for thirty years before moving to New Jersey. Her companion is Mexican, a language teacher who also gives cultural tours. Two minutes later, the three of us are lamenting the Gore fiasco and worrying about an undereducated fool becoming the most powerful man in the world. Her time in Patzcuaro is ending, the woman says; but there's no better guide to the city and region than Guillermo, her dinner companion.

Guillermo and I exchange cards. Of course, he knows the Casa and its owners, Czech-born artists now living in Vermont; he also knows their tenants, the Great River Arts Institute—the sponsors of my residency. In fact, Guillermo seems to know everyone of importance in Patzcuaro and many others, too. He promises to stop by at the Casa the following afternoon to work out a tutoring schedule.

Born in northern Mexico, which he refers to as Mexamerica, Guillermo bridges two cultures. For years his comfortable, well-educated parents sent him to summer camp in the U.S. He thanks the camp for his perfectly unaccented English. No matter how I try, I'll never achieve a similar mastery in Spanish (which I didn't begin studying until age nineteen) or in French, which I've been speaking, on infrequent occasions, since age seven. Our plan—Guillermo's and mine—is an hour of conversation at 4:00 p.m. every day on Mexican subjects: especially history, politics, and education. Good for my head as well as my ear, I tell myself.

The Friday pottery market gets good press in my guidebook and at the Casa. Ambling around, I see stacks of locally produced earthenware bowls and plates; they are evenly glazed (not always the case in Mexico's pottery pueblos) and reputed to be dishwasher safe. At least a dozen vendors are selling mugs and plates with bold floral designs, many with sunflowers. Kitsch Mexican, I would say.

I can't help wondering: Is some designer from *el Norte* promoting this commercially viable look? Have some of these artisans signed on with Walmart?

Around 1:00 p.m., I head for the internet café near the Plaza Grande. Grinning at the young guy who runs the place, I grab a seat at the second station (out of eight) in from the door. From my faithful correspondent in California and other friends, I receive the political news (no definitive word yet on Gore–Bush). But even more important, I'm peppered with questions related to my project. Who else is at the Casa? How's the food? The street life? Are the Plaza Grande and the Plaza Chica somewhat like Lincoln Center and Union Square? Where do you go for dinner (none is served at the Casa)? And with whom?

At the machine to my right, an American woman mulls over an email from her college-age daughter. She's either working too hard or too little, the mom tells me when she learns about my thirty-five years as a college professor. There's not much you can do, I say, except try not to give too much advice. On the other side is another Patzcuaro native, in his twenties. When he seems eager to chat, I ask about his work. He studied Business at a local college, Pedro tells me, and hopes to make a career in Hospitality. It's my time now, he says. Indeed, Patzcuaro's more fortunate young people are preparing for the global future. Pretty soon this educated cohort will all be on cell phones, like their counterparts in the States, chatting with friends and calling in video orders, plane tickets, and stock purchases.

The up-and-coming young are on my mind because I've been reading Thomas Friedman's *The Lexus and the Olive Tree*—on the challenges posed by late twentieth-century technology to traditional values and life-ways. Friedman's optimistic account of globalization (with the promise—some of it just visible—of an improved standard of living for people in Mexican pueblos, Chinese hamlets, and remote Tanzanian villages) is news I prefer to CNN reports of starvation, flooding, malaria deaths, and U.S. military exploits. Of course, Friedman reminds readers that we need "olive trees"—roots in community and culture—to balance the efficiency, growth, and high-tech represented by the Lexus in his title. Here in Patzcuaro, the rituals of the Day of the Dead link the living and the deceased through cemetery visits, home altars, and street theater. *Muertos*, as it's called, is a source of stability and a cherished identity.

Stability and mobility vie for my attention in Patzcuaro. Standing on line at a local bank, I talk to a Mexican worker in his forties who tells me that he picked grapes in California, apples in Washington State, and farmed potatoes using a tractor in Idaho. Which place did you like best? I ask. Idaho, he says. "Because of the tractor. I loved that machine." Is that the Lexus speaking? Or just a working man's dream of power? In another vein, the taxi driver who takes me from the airport in Morelia to Patzcuaro (a trip of about an hour) insists on speaking English all the way to the Casa. He worked in an electronics factory in Perth Amboy, New Jersey, he says, where the hours were long and the conditions often unpleasant. But he loved his time there and the freedom from family constraints. He shows me a small English grammar that he keeps in his cab. He consults it at least once every day, he says.

Ladina and Michael Pavlic, the absentee owners of the Casa,

stop by to check on some bills. They also own a modern house on Lake Patzcuaro, about a half-hour away. A friend, a Mexican sculptor who is half-Czech, joins them for a mezcal. I tell the Pavlics and their guest that I've been to the Czech Republic, twice as a visiting lecturer—and never managed to learn a single word of Czech. They understand. "No one picks up our language casually," Michael says. "It's not like Spanish—or mezcal." The Pavlics have their favorite mezcal dealer, Don Pedro, who brings them "the best stuff" in unmarked, gallon-sized jugs. Ladina enjoys a mezcal every day, "for her health," she tells me, and never has stomach troubles. Their stuff is smooth and a pleasure to drink. I could get hooked. . . .

Conclusions: Writing Away from Home

In Patzcuaro, I am liberated from running to Whole Foods for kale and radicchio salads, Israeli couscous, and barbecued chicken. I don't have to water my jade plants or buy more toilet paper. I'm free of the daily angst which comes from reading the *New York Times* first thing in the morning and listening to *The News Hour* on PBS before dinner. (There's no TV at the Casa.)

I love escaping my routines. But do I really have more free time at the Casa? I'm occupied, it turns out, prowling the same Patzcuaro streets, browsing almost daily in the same half-dozen craft and souvenir shops, and kibitzing with the same hippie venders. The spring-like weather draws me out. Mexican kitsch beckons. I buy a few Day of the Dead souvenirs: small skulls, two grinning skeletons (each about five inches tall) in chef's hats, and two playing the banjo and the flute; also incense, candles, and some black-and-white photos of the celebration. I visit a Purepecha museum with Guillermo and several galleries with Julie, an American artist who arrived at the Casa after I settled in. I spend three days going back and forth to Tzurumutaro, a Purepecha village twenty minutes from town, witnessing funeral ceremonies for Esperanza's father-in-law.

These experiences keep me scribbling. Writing helps me think about what's familiar in the seemingly unfamiliar. At the end of the funeral service, for example, there's a round of handshaking. Each of us turns to the left and then to the right and says, "*La paz, la paz*" (peace, peace). For a brief, seductive moment, I feel part of this warm (and unknown) community, grateful to be included, even as an outsider.

When I write to friends about the funeral, I can't help boasting about crossing over—being with Esperanza's family in their loss and then in the bonding which helps them get through it. But I exaggerate. I'm watching and I'm moved, but I'll leave in the evening. I'll leave them—whatever I might write about their grief, their loss, and their ways of being together. If there were postcards of such rituals, I'd buy a dozen and send them to friends and family in the States. If I took photographs—and I don't—I might do the same. Who can resist showing off such non-touristic connections to that Other World?

Everyday learning feels more intense, more significant, when the "classroom" is an unfamiliar place and the language of instruction is foreign. But where do such reactions lead? What kind of writing do they inspire?

Relax, I tell myself. Enjoy this seductive, low-cost vacation. During the cold dark days in *el Norte*, when even a coffee at Starbucks or a sauna at the nearby spa seems like too much trouble, there will be time to attack my notes.

May 2018: After a Long Absence

My original Patzcuaro Diary, written eighteen years ago, tells me more than I expected and not exactly what I expected. What's clearest is a sense of place—a place I would like my friends to know and my grown grandchildren to visit: a town where the weight of the past does not seem (underline *seem*) to be crushing the present, and where the present does not promise to destroy the past, a place where locals report good experiences north of the border and where we from *el Norte* feel safe and welcome.

That was then, I remind myself. What relation exists between this glowing report from the year 2000 and the present? How has Patzcuaro responded to the pressures of late capitalism, advances in technology, and Trump's anti-immigrant politics? Google, if I check, will tell me more than I want to know. My Patzcuaro stories have a precious specificity—like a soup that won't tolerate garlic, curry, or cream. They are a record of then. Nostalgia is their defining quality—and their limitation.

POST CARD: *DIA DE LOS MUERTOS* / DAY OF THE DEAD, MEXICO, 2000

Dear Ladina and Michael:

I've told you that my late husband Eli was a painter drawn to the theme of death. He was wry about the subject, in the Mexican manner. On paper and canvas, his male subjects—sometimes in death masks—tease the living with their manic energy and fearlessness. Let's defy death, they announce, as if ready to cavort (Mexican style) on their own graves. How he would have relished the celebration of The Day of the Dead in Patzcuaro!

Now I want to take a bit of Muertos *home with me: six small death masks made of sugar, and a pair of* caterinas *(skeletons) playing the banjo and the flute; two small incense burners and two tall yellow candles; some vivid black-and-white photos (8 x 10") of* Dia de los Muertos, *some with candles lit on Lake Patzcuaro; and a half dozen sheets of* papel picata *(cut paper) — in red, yellow, and pink—featuring saints, birds, and flowers.*

Around these decorations, I'll make a Muertos *party for Eli and his death paintings: next November, ideally on* Todos Santos, *on the first or second day of the month. A large table along one wall of his studio will* hold the ofrenda: *a display of pumpkins, gourds, and fruits of the season with a vase of marigolds on either side, and a sign reading* Drinks in the Front Room. *Guests will see a few of Eli's late self-portraits (grim heads acknowledging life's dark side) on the table and photos by our friend Carol Kitman capturing the exuberant man he also was. We'll feast on mezcal, spicy* pozole, *chocolate-caramel flan, and Mexican bread from a local baker. If only you could be with us.*

Abrazos,

Doris

GEORGIA, NOT THE PEACH STATE, 2002

PRIL, 2002. AFTER A SIX-HOUR LAYOVER at London/
Heathrow and with only a limited interest in duty-free
liquor, I join passengers for Tbilisi (Georgia) and Yere-
van (Armenia) on a queue at Gate 17. No announcement is made
about our British Air flight 6721, and the light at Gate 17 remains
dark as we board. However, the folks on line—including several
embassy and NGO employees—seem untroubled. Traveling to the
Caucuses is like this, they say.

After settling into my seat, I turn to *The Constant Gardner*, John
le Carré's novel about a pharmaceutical giant that falsifies drug tri-
als in Africa and murders the whistle-blowers—in collusion with
the British Foreign Service and the British Secret Service. Five
hours later, deplaning in Tbilisi in the midnight rain, I struggle to
release myself from the grip of le Carré's tale of conspiracy and cor-
ruption. My Georgian colleagues, with more troubles in this arena
than I can possibly imagine, will be looking to me for American op-
timism, not twenty-first-century cynicism and despair.

ON MY SECOND MORNING IN TBILISI, I am sitting in the sleek, marble lobby of the Hotel Primavera, waiting for Vaso to pick me up. The seven-month-old Primavera, with a fully equipped gym in the basement and a covered rooftop pool, both rare in post-Communist Georgia, is a joint venture between Georgian and U.S. investors. The lobby is empty at 9:45 a.m. except for the pale, dark-eyed young woman with an elegant neck straight out of Modigliani, who sits behind the reception desk.

Watching the narrow street, I see a police car slip into a space just beyond the hotel entrance. Thirty seconds later, a black Mercedes stops at the door, discharging three young guys in black leather jackets and a man in his forties wearing a tweed jacket and slacks. From the opposite side of the street, three other men, also in black leather jackets, rush to greet these four with handshakes and kisses; they then step aside as the four, following the fellow in the tweed jacket, enter the hotel. A second black Mercedes pulls up behind the first one, and a second group of four emerges. Again, there are handshakes and kisses all around; again, the four enter the Primavera, this time with a silver-haired man in a navy suit, white shirt, and blue silk tie in the lead. A quarter of an hour later, the eight men march back through the lobby and into the street. They pile into the two Mercedes sedans and trail a police escort out to the boulevard.

Is this *The Godfather* I'm seeing? Or some version of le Carré's pharma-thugs in action? Did the two principal players cut a deal about miracle pain killers or poppy-based drugs? Or did they meet a third player, already within, to talk finance or construction? Did money change hands? Was there a payoff for the cops? In a country where sixty percent of the economy is gray market, where cops need to be on the take to eat and university professors need three jobs to pay the rent, this is surely business as usual. Or is it? Will I ever find out what I have witnessed?

Even more important: what difference would my knowing make? I'm here in the Caucuses—wedged between Russia, Armenia, and Turkey—to lecture about Diversity in American Culture, the Challenge of 9/11, and the U.S. Response to a Changing World. In between my talks, with luck, I'll learn what I can about my hosts and the world they inhabit.

"TWO DAYS AFTER THE ATTACK ON SEPTEMBER 11," I tell an audience of seventy-five students and faculty, "I had a curious dream. I was standing with Hillary Clinton, who said to me, on the verge of tears, 'So much was invested in these buildings.'" In the dream, Hillary pointed to Ground Zero, the devastated sixteen acres upon which the World Trade Center once stood. I don't need a psychoanalyst to point out that the dream was about mourning our losses, and that Hillary was speaking for me.

"Invested" is a key word here. The Twin Towers were about money—about the evolution of global capitalism into the dominant system in the world today. Americans weren't the only victims of the attack. More than four hundred companies from twenty-eight nations had offices at the World Trade Center; people from eighty countries worked there. Not a big happy family, of course: rather a combination of high-living professionals and underpaid immigrant service workers. "Inequality and interdependence," I note, "are with us in the ashes of the World Trade Center. Whatever our enemies are saying, can we Americans learn from this tragedy? Can we do better?"

Anyone in the audience expecting an answer from me will be disappointed. I close by confessing that I run away from the problem, several times a week, to the steam room at my health club. There I hope to find a Korean woman who told me when we first met that she's a magician. Some weeks later I discovered that the woman, who plays the harp in a New York orchestra, is actually a musician. Understanding one another across cultures, even when people live on the same suburban street, is challenging. "I could use a magician here in Tbilisi," I confess. "Are there any volunteers?"

"WE'VE GOT SOMETHING DIFFERENT on the schedule today," my colleague Tina says. "A change of pace from American Studies." Indeed. Our destination is Gori, thirty miles away, where Stalin was born to a shoemaker and his wife, and where the Georgians have built a museum in his honor. It's odd, Tina confesses, to see the people of Gori so attached to a brutal dictator, their famous native son. "Stalin built the Soviet state—occupying a sixth of the earth—and put his home town prominently on the map of the world."

The museum is a drab palazzo: six plain rooms filled with photographs and newspaper articles documenting Stalin's rise from simple beginnings to world leader. I learn his real, Georgian name: Iosit (Soso) Dzhughashvili. Of course, there's no mention of the deaths, famines, or people displaced as a result of his policies. What did I expect?

Noticing the museum gift shop, I smile. Ah, yes: kitschy key chains, maybe luggage tags, buttons, or blank notebooks with Stalin's picture on the front—mementos certain to amuse friends at home. But no. Except for a few books in Georgian and Russian, there's nothing to purchase. Ah, the frustrations of the traveler as shopper. "We Georgians are still worrying about food, clothing, shelter, and education," Tina explains. "Museum souvenirs aren't a priority."

TEN DAYS INTO MY VISIT, after the keynote address, several small presentations, and many receptions, I'm weary of formalities. I've been watching my words, watching my wine-consumption, and smiling non-stop. Now I'm anticipating the question that a Tbilisi journalist is almost certain to ask me: "When will you return to Georgia?" It's tempting to respond, *When the government and university authorities show enough respect for students and teachers to provide them with decent bathrooms.* Bathrooms are an issue for Georgians: They are dark, smelly, rarely cleaned, and without any available paper. But okay: I'll be on my way home in four more days. Why am I fussing?

I get through the interview without embarrassing my government or myself. It's not easy to play the candid American—even if my goal is to mock my own attitudes and locate the privileged perspective from which I speak. Still, I want the fifty students in the audience to hear an honest, cranky, and self-mocking answer. Being real is important in part because I have just given a forty-minute talk on "How We Live Now," about the complexities and contradictions of American multiculturalism. "At my health club," I said, returning to my favorite example, "Korean women throw their used towels on the floor for the Latina housekeepers to pick up. Then the Koreans wonder why the Latinas are more gracious to 'White' women than to them." Bathrooms, like garbage collection and wine production, are cultural data. They tell us things we know, would rather not know, and often seem beyond our control. If only we Americans could be as attentive to the needs of the homeless and hungry as we are to the cleanliness of our bathrooms.

PROBABLY R. HAD BEEN DRINKING when he called me from Kansas. No, that's wrong. When the phone rang it was Sunday morning, May 12—ten days after I had been a guest on his campus. "Happy Mother's Day," he said, the heavy accent and the greeting momentarily at odds. He was at the state university, he explained, to sign an exchange agreement and was eager to know whether the end of my Georgian trip had gone smoothly.

Of course, in celebration of the agreement, R. had probably had several glasses of wine the night before. Maybe when he settled into his hotel room on Saturday evening, stirred by alcohol, he re-played the dinner party he'd hosted in my honor. He would have remembered the emotional round of toasts: to new friends, to friendship between our two countries, to our children, to love, to doing our work with love. . . . Round and round the table we had gone, as is the Georgian custom, each toast more shamelessly sentimental than the previous one.

Toasting in Georgia is social cement. Wine frees Georgians to speak emotionally: to celebrate their nation, their precious language, and the fruits of their rich soil—the eggplants, walnuts, tomatoes, and greens, the grapes and melons, the tradition of wine-making and their own homemade wines. Men become tender and even tearful about their parents and their children. They invite strangers into their intimate circle. I was easily seduced.

Our party of eight was alone that night in a spacious restaurant along the river's edge. The service was attentive and dignified. First came the cold vegetable salads, the cold meats, dumplings, and smoked fish; then garlicky chicken, baked sturgeon, sliced pork, and the famous Georgian cheese pie, served hot in a pastry dough. Sentimental Georgian music blared over the speaker system. Maybe R. remembered the two of us dancing a slow two-step while the others at our table watched or tried not to watch or imagined scenarios which would have no basis in fact.

R. and I did not become lovers. But there was a sympathy between us. I let him know that I appreciated his skill and sweetness with his faculty and his graciousness toward me. He let me know how much he admired my lectures. And my looks.

A few months after I returned home, R. wrote to ask a favor. He was hosting a conference on "America in the World" and wondered if I would write an opening comment for him. While I couldn't quite manage the ghost-writing, R.'s request loosened my tongue. Here's what I as an American might say, I wrote to R:

What a strange, troubled time this is in the U.S. The American President, the archetypal Lone Ranger and world's self-appointed Top Cop, has announced that "we are the best nation on the face of the earth." He confidently makes this claim as the U.S. fights undeclared wars, models sleazy capitalism, ignores poverty at home, boosts global warming

*abroad, and produces gas-guzzling SUVs while lamenting U.S. depend-
ence on Middle East oil. Yes, one year after 9/11—after the shock and
the sorrow, after displays of deep reflection—the public face of America
seems unblemished. Maybe it's those injections of botox, removing wrin-
kles while freezing expressiveness.*

Did R. make use of my candor? He never said, and it doesn't
matter. I added the note to my folder marked *Georgia* and tucked
the folder away in a drawer.

POST CARD: WELCOME, MR. JAMES BOND, GERMANY, 2015

*D*EPLANING IN BERLIN ON A COOL OCTOBER MORNING, *Paul pulls on his battered trench coat—with the epaulettes still in place —and collects our bags. In the cab, he tests his basic German* (es geht gut) *and nods in relief. My silver-haired companion is primed for ten busy days to come. At our hotel, Dieter behind the desk grins as he glances at Paul's passport. "Welcome, Mr. Bond," he exclaims. "Room 007 awaits you!"*

I catch Dieter giving me a quick once-over: a tall, lean woman in black with dangling silver earrings. Yes, a decent companion for James.

Indeed, Room 007 is a singular space. In addition to sleeping quarters, the suite includes a large living room—dining room and a kitchen area with a refrigerator and a microwave. And one additional feature: a view of the hotel's tranquil, not quite secret inner garden.

When we leave the hotel, our Mr. Bond has his own spying agenda: checking on the remnants of The Wall, examining the redone State Opera and the Babelplatz, and meeting an old professor for drinks at the Adlon. Then there's a Rendezvous with History at the Denkmal fur die Enmordeten Juden (The Holocaust Museum). It's seventy years since the end of the War. The Germans, I say, have chosen to live honorably with their past. Avoiding euphemisms, they confess to murdering millions of Jews. My spy nods solemnly. "Remembering their evil deeds," he adds, "they will not repeat them."

PASSOVER WITH THE SAMARITANS, PALESTINE, 2010

NABIL AND I, ALONG WITH SOME THREE THOUSAND other visitors (Israelis, Palestinians, and foreigners), peer down from makeshift bleachers onto a field the size of a basketball court. Religious leaders in Turkish-style red hats (wrapped with bands of white cloth or straw) and green silk robes dominate the space. I listen as they chant blessings and holiday prayers in an almost familiar Hebrew—or a linguistic first cousin. Surrounding them—and joining in prayer—are more than a hundred Samaritan men and boys, dressed in tall rubber boots, white warm-up pants, white sweatshirts, and white baseball caps. It's April 28, 2010, according to the "Western" calendar, and the beginning of the Samaritan Passover.

The phrase "Good Samaritan" is familiar from the New Testament parable—about a traveler who is beaten, left to die, and then rescued by a stranger, a Samaritan. The Samaritans, I discover, are descendants of Abraham with practices linked to Jewish history and traditions. They have built their religion around four principles: one God (of Israel), one prophet (Moses), one holy text (the first five books of Moses), and one holy place (Mount Gerizim), where we have come to witness this ceremony.

Mount Gerizim, the Samaritans believe, is the authentic Mount Sinai: the site where Abraham prepared to sacrifice his son Isaac. As recounted in Genesis, when God saw Abraham's obedience to his divine will, he ordered him to spare his son and kill a lamb instead. The Samaritans came to live on Mount Gerizim more than thirty-five hundred years ago. Their ancient Passover tradition celebrates freedom from bondage with the ritual sacrifice of lambs.

Of course, such a long history, including conversions among their "tribe" to Christianity and Islam, is rarely an easy one. Required to marry within their community, the Samaritans are a dying breed. Only seven hundred remain. Of that number, four hundred reside in Kiryat Luza, just below Mount Gerizim, at the top of the West Bank city of Nablus. The rest live in Holon, near Tel Aviv. Many Samaritans *look* familiar to me—like Israeli Ashkenazi Jews or American Jews. I see their faces on the Upper West Side of Manhattan, on the streets of Teaneck and Tenafly, and in the photo albums of both sides of my family.

Nabil Alawi is my guide and host. My talk with his students two days ago ended with food and how it divides us from one another—except when it doesn't. Now, he's offering me a once-in-a-lifetime glimpse of Samaritan rituals, food, and culture, which I'll be savoring (and digesting) for some long time to come.

After thirty minutes of chanting, the main action begins: the ritual slaughter, followed by preparations for the Passover meal and the days ahead. Teams of fathers and sons draw close to their patient, year-old lambs. Then the men team up: a pair, using minimal force, holds down each of the lambs as the third looks the animal in the eye and aims the eighteen-inch blade of his knife at the jugular. The lambs do not cry out; in fact, they barely struggle. The boys, standing beside their fathers, watch attentively—without fear or flinching or chatter.

I wonder: Did a few of the youngest boys weep last night, pleading with their fathers to spare the innocent animals? And if there was such an effort at intercession, did the fathers respond with kindness? Or impatience? The poise of all the players is mysterious to me. What keeps the lambs so calm? Have they been given a tranquilizer this morning with their drinking water?

Following the slaughter, the men rejoice. Clapping their hands above their heads, they dance a few steps before kissing one another. Their exultation—and perhaps relief at putting the killing behind them—is contagious. The Samaritan women also clap vigorously; they laugh, smile, hug their children and one another.

Next, the men, with blood on their hands, move out of the killing field to embrace their wives, daughters, and friends. I watch them gently place a drop of blood on the foreheads of family members, thus including them in the ritual and its blessings. Surely, as in the *Seder* I know, the sign of blood indicates that these are the "holy ones" to be "passed over" by the Angel of Death—or spared other manifestations of God's vengeance.

The last phase of the ceremony, preparing the animals for cooking, seems to take mere minutes. The slaughterers, moving with practiced efficiency, skin, clean, and skewer the lambs; then they carry them to nearby barbecue pits, where fires are already burning. The lambs will cook through the night.

I ask Nabil how the Samaritans fare among West Bank Arabs. He has friends in the community and chats with a few of them as we move through the crowd. While their script is like Hebrew but different, Nabil explains, the Samaritans have embraced Arabic as their first language. This allows for relatively easy blending (except for marriage) into everyday life on the West Bank. Samaritan students attend his university. "They seem comfortable on their cultural tightrope," I say.

"It's all very complicated," Nabil responds, "like everything else in our small corner of the globe."

"COMPLICATED," I KNOW, IS AN UNDERSTATEMENT. Whether uttered by an Arab or an Israeli (and doubtless by a Samaritan as well), the word hides ancient hatreds along with everyday anxieties about safety and survival. "Complicated" camouflages not only rage but despair. When I travel from Tel Aviv to Nablus, my Israeli taxi driver, a retired military officer, confesses to nervousness about entering the West Bank. "Are you afraid?" he asks me.

Afraid? The question catches me by surprise. An invitation to visit Nabil's university prompted this trip to Israel. Being there, in Nablus—not in Tel Aviv or Jerusalem, where I've been before—is the experience I crave; it's the story I'm itching to write. "Your passenger is a naive American," I tell the driver. "I'm not afraid, even though I probably should be."

When the taxi deposits me at the grim military checkpoint attached to a large parking lot, Israeli soldiers inspect my passport and grill me about my "mission" in the Occupied Territory. Waiting for Nabil to pick me up, I imagine how Palestinians must feel crossing into Israel. The hostile reception they receive from soldier-gatekeepers is meant to discourage their movements—to work, to seek medical care, for cultural events or family gatherings. The ritual at the border underscores the Palestinians' second-class status. It fuels their rage.

Driving up the mountain with Nabil, from Nablus where he lives to Mount Gerizim, is surprisingly simple: no checkpoints, no police roadblocks, and no worries about entering another country. The Samaritans, who have Israeli citizenship, appear to live confidently on the West Bank. Perhaps it's the protective presence of Mount Gerizim that keeps them calm and balanced.

I think about how faith transforms acts of carnage into devotional experiences—and how faith sustains these Samaritans. Even as their numbers shrink. Even as the number of tourists for these Passover ceremonies is almost ten times the size of their tiny community. I wonder: Do many eighteen-year old Samaritans dream of studying in Israel at the Technion or the Hebrew University? Do some actually enroll? In the Age of the Internet, what happens to such vulnerable communities? How much attrition can the Samaritans withstand?

POST CARD: THE JEWS OF DJERBA, TUNISIA, 1979

I'M WATCHING TWO MEN IN SOFT-WHITE DRAWSTRING PANTS *and collarless tops standing before the Temple ark, lost in the passion of prayer. Raising their arms, they rotate and sway, holding aloft an enormous prayer shawl. A dozen other men and boys, all with their shoes off, sit cross-legged on blue-green tile benches covered with straw mats. The boys, not to be outdone by their fathers and uncles, sing along passionately, giving themselves over to the ritual.*

Eli, standing next to me, reaches automatically for the camera in his shoulder bag. But then he catches himself—no photos in a house of worship. Regrouping, he studies the two men on the bima *and their other-worldly dance with the prayer shawl. They seem ready to levitate, as if on the verge of flying with God. Can I hold onto this spiritual frenzy? he worries. The sense of these men as God-possessed? Shall I paint them as weightless? Fed by faith?*

Djerba, an island separated by an inlet from the Tunisian mainland, is renowned for its ancient Jewish community. In the town of Houmt Souk, they prospered as goldsmiths. Now only a few modest jewelry stores remain. Their synagogue, la Griba, long a pilgrimage site for North

African Jews, seems eerily quiet, almost forgotten. Within the past year, friends in Tunis tell us, some Arabs set fire to the place. Now members of the Jewish community live more carefully among their neighbors, alert to signs of danger and the rekindling of religious acrimony.

I wonder about the absence of women on the premises of the synagogue. Do they pray at home? Are prayer and levitation reserved for men while women fetch wood for fire and cook the Sabbath meal—and all those other meals, too?

A TALE OF THREE *ZA'TARS*, ISRAEL / PALESTINE, 2010

B RACHA AND MOSHE, MY FRIEND BATYA'S COUSINS in the suburbs of Tel Aviv, greet us with candid political commentary. Their aggressive, expansionist government is "shitty," they announce. What a relief! While Batya adores these Israeli cousins, I wasn't sure how their politics (and some inevitable political differences) might color our ten days together. Of course, the Israelis worry about the security of a country they cherish and don't wish to abandon. They also worry about whether we'll be safe, across the border in Jordan on a trip to Petra, and the risks I'll be taking—foolishly, they believe—during a three-day visit to the West Bank.

The orthodox in Jerusalem, we learn, are trying to segregate city buses (men in the front, women in the back) but haven't yet succeeded. Palestinians watch helplessly as Israeli settlers build new towns in their territory. Israelis and Palestinians feel similarly unloved and at risk. However, to a non-religious Jewish visitor from the U.S., the Israeli lament seems disproportionate. At almost every turn, I see signs of stunning prosperity along with scientific and military prowess; the Palestinians, I know, struggle with inept governance and a spliced-up land. Of course, everyone I speak to claims to want peace, but nobody mentions the compromises needed to get there.

Day after day, in Israel, Jordan, and the West Bank, I eat the same perfect tomatoes, crunchy cucumbers, excellent tabbouleh, flavorful humus, lightly floral olive oil—and no pork. Among the pleasures of this common cuisine is *za'tar*—a spice mix, principally thyme, with sesame seeds, sumac, cumin, oregano, and salt added. It's used on flatbreads for "pizzas" and mixed with olive oil for dipping. *Za'tar* "pizzas" are omnipresent at Arab breakfasts and on Israeli fast-food stands.

IN THE GALILEE, ABOUT AN HOUR NORTH OF HAIFA, we stay overnight at a Druze B and B. The Druze are a distinctive Arab community, loyal to the State of Israel, and the only Arabs to serve in the Israeli army. The owners, a high-energy young couple, welcome our party of six (including Batya's cousins and two of their friends) as if we were all well acquainted. We sit down to an overloaded dinner table—including a vivid watercress salad, featherlight pita breads, and *za'tar* mixed with olive oil for dipping. Platters of roast lamb, baked chicken, rice, stuffed grape leaves, and sautéed eggplant surround the lighter fare.

The next morning, we are treated to a repeat performance—but without the chicken and lamb. Breakfast, we all agree, featuring freshly baked pitas with *za'tar* along with seven or eight salads, is even better than dinner. The pita/pizzas, warm from the oven and crunchy with *za'tar*, are the stars of the meal.

A few hours later, in the Galilee near Kibbutz Dafna, we stop at a site marking the 1997 crash of two Israeli helicopters. Seventy-three young fighters perished in a training exercise. The memorial includes a shady arbor with seventy-three small, thin wood boards hanging from trees, each bearing a name. At the entrance to the site, a slab of gray stone is engraved with the names and home towns of the dead. Nearby, in an open field, seventy-three oddly anthropomorphic, reddish-gold stones, each about four feet tall and different from the others, exude an otherworldly presence.

A short distance from the field of stones, I spot a table covered with a white cloth. Standing behind it are two local women selling their own *za'tar*. "The *za'tar* comes from our fields," the younger woman says. "From this earth." In a jiffy I buy a small fat jar, maybe two inches high; and then I buy a second.

IN NABLUS THE FOLLOWING WEEK, I visit my American Studies colleague Nabil Alawi and his family. A professor of English in his mid fifties, Nabil has a Ph.D. from the University of Tennessee. His wife and their four kids (sixteen to twenty-two) all speak fluent English with me. Alas, I have no Arabic to offer them.

Nablus is a vertical city with high-rise apartment buildings, mostly white concrete, defining the landscape. An Najah University, sprawling, modern, and high up on one of the hills, enrolls twenty thousand students. The ancient lower city features a crumbling, meandering *souk*. At every turn, I notice shops piled high with cheap shoes and plastic goods. Blond manikins decorate the doorways. What happened, I wonder, to the old craftsmen—the silversmiths and weavers, incense and perfume makers—now nowhere in sight? Nabil points out four different places where Israeli soldiers have shot and killed Palestinians.

When we emerge from the *souk*, I follow Nabil into a local spice shop. In English, I ask about *za'tar*. Immediately, the shopkeeper brings me an overflowing scoop of the spice mixture from an enormous canvas sack sitting against the back wall. "Can I smell it?" I surprise myself by asking. Clearly the same as in Israel—at least to my untutored nose. I buy a half kilo, divided into two plastic bags, each double wrapped.

The next day, cheered by my second *za'tar* purchase and the sweetness of Nabil's family, I speak informally with some forty-five students of English. Nabil has organized this "event" at the last moment, he tells me. I am delighted—both to meet Palestinian students, and to be spared the effort of writing a carefully nuanced talk for the occasion. When he introduces me, Nabil tells his students that I have been traveling in Jordan (true enough) but avoids mentioning Israel.

The students' focus is on Obama: Why won't he just give the Palestinians their state, they ask. I relax: This is easy enough for openers. I explain that the American president can't dictate to the U.S., no less to the rest of the world. I speak a bit about Obama the idealist and visionary, and Obama the politician and pragmatist. I mention the powerful forces constraining him at home and abroad. But mostly, I listen as students make long, generally polite speeches about American imperialism and Israeli militarism and racism. In their place, I would do no less.

Towards the end of the session, Nabil asks me to say something about my food memoir (*Eating as I Go: Scenes from America and Abroad*,

2006) and matters of food and culture. "Historic enemies who are neighbors, like the Greeks and the Turks, and who share the same soil and climate," I say, "often eat the same foods. Like the Israelis and Palestinians." Wait, really? I seem to have shocked my audience with what I assumed is common knowledge about their "neighbor." But isn't. The students are even more surprised to learn that Arab food is readily available—and familiar to non-Arab shoppers—in many parts of the U.S. "Couscous is stocked in ordinary supermarkets as well as in gourmet shops," I say, "but *za'tar* is tricky to find."

A day later, on the way back to Israel from Nablus, with the bags of *za'tar* in my carry-on, I realize that the stuff is aggressively perfuming my clothes. Plastic, even double bags, may contain the seeds but not their smell. Anyone opening my suitcase would know I am smuggling spices.

Some secrets are harder to keep than others—and more important to keep. Our Israeli hosts warn me before leaving for the airport (and the U.S.) not to say anything about visiting the West Bank. Israeli security might think I was spying. They make me uneasy about the *za'tar*. Too much risk, I tell myself, especially for a risk-averse traveler. I decide to leave the Palestinian *za'tar* with Bracha and Moshe, even as I suspect that they will reject it as "other." If you can't use it, I say, give it to your housekeeper (an Arab woman). Or throw it away.

U.S. Customs now forbids anything and everything edible— even seeds—from entering the country. On my Customs form, I declared nothing. At 6:00 a.m., on arrival at JFK, I notice that none of the Customs officials is asking U.S. citizens to open bags.

Had I been a touch paranoid? Or simply sensible about the uncertainties of world travel?

AT HOME IN MY LEONIA KITCHEN, I divide half of my *za'tar* stash into three little spice jars for gifts. And I obsess about the *za'tar* I've left behind. What a perfect gift for many close friends—and if I'm lucky, still a possible one. Indeed, I can buy *za'tar* in multi-ethnic New Jersey. In fact, I will buy *za'tar*, right away, for my own use. And maybe to give away—with a real or false background story, depending upon the occasion and my mood.

Three days after my return, before heading into the city for a small dinner party, I stop at Joeyness, a Lebanese-American take-out in Fort Lee. I'm especially fond of the shop's organic, freshly made soups—and I welcome a coffee "on the house" while my order is being filled. Joey, the chef-owner and a graduate of the Culinary Institute of America, presides amiably over the stove and ovens in the rear; his mother lavishes Middle Eastern charm on a stream of regular customers. She's at the front counter when I appear. "Do you sell *za'tar*," I ask.

"No," she replies. "But I could let you have some—for a fancy price." She opens a huge container, announcing, "It's from Lebanon," and begins spooning the spice into a 4-ounce plastic jar.

"Wait—how much?" I ask.

"For you," she smiles, "it's free." I immediately buy a quart of my favorite pea soup with mint (for ten dollars) and head down the hill to Leonia.

At the Brownsteins, on the Upper West Side, I expect to be grilled on Israeli politics and my Palestinian adventures. Perhaps *za'tar* will connect the two realms. I've brought as a house gift half of the Joeyness *za'tar*, repacked in a squat Israeli jar. "A souvenir from Israel," I say when Shale opens the door. After several glasses of wine and Rachel's Middle Eastern chicken with chickpeas, I recount the tale of three *za'tars*. But I do not mention that *their za'tar* is not from Israel. And not from Palestine. I keep silent, knowing that both Rachel and Shale would be entertained by the idea that I have substituted Lebanese *za'tar*, bought in New Jersey, for the Israeli-grown product, which is the same as the Palestinian-grown product.

The same? Shale, delighting in such conundrums, would probably have insisted that the Lebanese, with their experience of French imperialism, produce a more nuanced *za'tar*—or a more corrupt one. Or, if Netanyahu had not been in the news for the past few days, he would have linked Israel's well-irrigated soil to a richer, bolder product. In truth, by the time *za'tar* enters the conversation, I am happily boozed and quite tired. My biggest concern is locating my parked car on Riverside Drive and making my way over the Bridge and home to Leonia.

POST CARD: THE SINGING
KEYNOTER, JAPAN, 1995

NOBODY WEARS JEANS OR SNEAKERS. *Dark suits are the uniform for men, stockings and heels for women, at the annual meeting of the Japanese Association for American Studies. Our contingent of five American professors has joined two hundred Japanese scholars in Sendai (four and a half hours north of Tokyo) to consider "The U.S. and Japan: Fifty Years After the End of the War." What simmers beneath the surface of Japanese wealth and well-being? I wonder. How does a nation, defeated in war, feel about the victors? How critical are "feelings" for these experts on U.S. politics and culture?*

The Plenary Session, one of only three conducted in English, features an address by the President of the American Studies Association, Paul Lauter. I watch Paul approach the podium in his navy suit, white shirt, and red-orange print tie. Does the tie suggest a touch of mischief?

Paul leans into the mike and signals for the slides to begin. We're looking at a corner of the Bronx, now crime-ridden, where the speaker attended junior high school during the War. On screen next is his Junior High School Song Book, his text for reading American culture at war. "Anchors Away, my boys," Paul sings—yes, he's singing—before comment-

ing on the naive enthusiasm with which his classmates celebrated combat. His next song, "From the Halls of Montezuma to the Shore of Tripoli," sounds, at this remove, more like a critique of imperialism than an embrace of militarism. The Japanese are caught off guard by this savvy and self-mocking performance. "America, the Beautiful" won the war, but the singing keynoter has softened the sting of victory.

AMBOS MUNDOS, CUBA, 2012

THE NAME OF OUR HOTEL, Ambos Mundos ("both worlds"), suggests a laudable ambition: to be a comfortable home-away-from-home for tourists while evoking the spirit and mores of urbane Cuba. Ninety years after it was constructed in the heart of Havana Vieja, the hulking six-story building displays the good bones, professional make-up, and proud bearing of an aging society matron. The impeccably painted, bright, deep salmon exterior and contrasting crisp white trim on the windows and balconies elicit admiring glances—and respect.

Inside is another story. The lobby—with a lovingly polished bar—is hot, stuffy, and AC-free. What's more, there are no ceiling fans to take the edge off the humid air. Scandinavian sofas and club chairs, circa 1960 and upholstered in orange linen, show signs of hard wear and guests distracted by drink.

Invisible in the lobby, but real to those in residence, are other indicators of age: toilets that need constant tweaking and can't be properly fixed because the American parts (now more than a half century old) are no longer made or are unavailable thanks to the (harassing and debilitating) U.S. boycott. In a similar vein, the showers sputter and drip, failing to deliver the steady volume of water that most tourists expect. The worthy lady's inner organs are a mess.

Still, I'm not sorry to be staying at Ambos Mundos. Nor are most of the thirty-five members of our group—mostly people in the arts and fans of my New Jersey City University colleague Ben Jones, our leader. We have come to learn about the island and enjoy the Eleventh Havana (Arts) Biennial. Right beyond the hotel's front door is the Obispo, a throbbing pedestrian thoroughfare and a location to be relished. Unfortunately, the location is not an asset when we're in transit. The big tourist buses that transport us from the airport and back can't get within six blocks of the place. So we arrive and depart like a ragtag troupe of street performers: following two bent, straining porters who push jerry-built dollies with our bags stacked six wobbly feet high.

Street life on the Obispo, which runs through the heart of Havana Vieja, offers us a non-stop, multi-media spectacle. Live music explodes out of every bar and restaurant; old men hawk their newspapers in singsong, and I take in the rhythms of the most rapidly spoken Spanish on the planet. Handsome Cuban "Re-enactors" in early twentieth-century dress approach tourists for a chat and a tip. Crowds gather to watch mimes frozen in seemingly impossible poses. Women with worn faces plead for soap or small change, and I remind myself to keep a supply of coins in my pocket. Through the window of a storefront school, I marvel at nine-year-olds in neat uniforms who seem completely focused on their teacher. Locals line up in front of a tiny pizzeria that I'm told does not sell to tourists. Passing a street bar, I breathe in the aroma of strong Cuban espresso.

Many afternoons, crowds of men standing three deep gather in front of an open double doorway, which is the side entrance to Ambos Mundos. Silent one moment and shouting and stomping the next, they're watching the National Pastime on a TV at the far end of the bar. In Cuba, it appears that no male over the age of five is indifferent to *baisbol*. The hotel accommodates this obsession, never chasing the baseball-mad fans from their positions. In fact, no one seems disturbed when the doormen and elevator operators drift away from their posts to catch their favorite players at bat or check on the score.

When I weary of this visual extravaganza and cacophony, the hotel provides a priceless escape. I take the ninety-year-old Otis elevator—a wrought iron cage with a heavy metal door that requires free hands and some muscle tone to push open and pull closed—to the sprawling sixth-floor terrace. From this perch, looking down at the deteriorating red clay rooftops, I contemplate the old city's handsome colonial heritage, laundry routines, and the romance of architectural ruins.

MORNINGS ON THE TERRACE, where a buffet breakfast is served, members of our group linger at glass-topped tables, relishing days that are ours to schedule. Over fruit salad, eggs, French toast, and weak coffee, we chat about museum-going, whether searching for an internet cafe is worth the trouble, the cost of food (inexpensive), and our favorites among the Biennial artists on the edge. Of course, we compare notes about the critical business of changing money. It's strictly a cash economy for tourists. There are no ATMs at hotels, and credit cards issued by American banks are not accepted anywhere. Further, while Cubans use the peso, we tourists are relegated to CUCs (Cuban convertible pesos), available only on the island, which allows the government tight control over foreign money along with stiff exchange fees.

In the late afternoon, after some hours of grappling with the heat between visits to museums and rounds of art and trinket shopping, I'm eager to return to the terrace. As dusk settles over the city and street lights shimmer, my companions and I drink Cristal, the delicious Cuban national beer, or Mojitos, the national drink, made with white rum, sugar, soda, and generous sprigs of mint. A multi-lingual buzz (I hear German, Italian, and Japanese along with Castilian and Argentinian Spanish) mixes easily with live Cuban music. More points for Ambos Mundos.

The hotel was, famously, Ernest Hemingway's Havana watering hole. Every winter, from 1932 to 1939, when he married Martha Gellhorn and bought a country house in the hills, he occupied Room 515. The Hemingway saga draws in the tourists, especially Americans. A mini-museum has been established in 515, and a "curator" is on hand, five days a week, to talk with visitors about the author of *The Sun Also Rises* and *A Farewell to Arms*. Hemingway, she tells me in English, was already a celebrity, thanks to those novels, when he first settled into Ambos Mundos. "*En Espanol, por favor,*" I say, not wanting to be taken for a monolingual American.

His room, small and bright, has a single bed (how did such a big guy, who probably never slept alone, manage?), a narrow writing table, and a couple of slim bookcases. On display are framed photos, copies of his novels, pens, his favorite corkscrews, and other para-phernalia of the writing and drinking life. Hemingway was a con-noisseur of wines and whiskey, the curator announces, really very knowledgeable. Well, yes, I know all about that storied piece of his life—and its impact, especially on his women. Amusing though it is to think of Hemingway at Ambos Mundos, the room-as-museum seems too modest and too neat for such an immodest and messy American personality. I would have appreciated a typewriter or at least a wastebasket full of discarded typed pages; also the smell of those iconic cigars—and everything they suggest about the habits of this writer and his obsessive dramas of masculinity.

ONE MORNING, AS MY STEPDAUGHTER SHOLA AND I are leav-ing our room, we notice four pairs of legs in dirty jeans dangling in front of our balcony. Closer inspection reveals house painters with their brushes and buckets of paint. In fact, we saw these men at breakfast, gathering their ropes and preparing to tie themselves to metal studs on the roof. Opening the French doors, I ask them if painting is an occasional job, or if they do this work regularly. "All the time," they say. "We have to keep painting and repainting the building." Maybe it's the humidity. Maybe it's the dirt that's spewed into the air all over town by thousands of 1950s Fords, Chevys, and Buicks— some beautifully preserved, and others held together by tape and a prayer.

Watching the painters dangle in front of our window, I think about Cuba in this (almost) transitional moment. The old *Fidelista* order produced widespread equality along with free, high-quality education and health care. For decades, Cuba flourished, thanks in part to financial support from the Soviet Union (until the break-up in 1990) and in spite of the U.S. boycott, which effectively cut off trade and normal exchange. Now, as is commonly acknowledged, Cubans suffer from crumbling buildings, restricted travel, imports in short supply, a weak technology sector, and extreme dependence on tourism.

There will be changes as the Castro brothers pass into history and a more globalized economy beckons. Tourist companies have already managed to bring in new cars, to be leased to visitors; and some lucky Cubans have received permission to buy their homes and sell their vehicles. Around the country, intimate family-owned restaurants (*paladares*)—and some not so intimate—licensed by the government, are luring tourists with the novelty of a comfy domestic atmosphere and profits for the owners. There's talk of small-scale entrepreneurship as a way to attract more tourist dollars and inject more vitality into the economy.

What lies ahead? The painters at Ambos Mundos, suspended from the rooftop, are in the maintenance business—gussying up the facade of a deteriorating structure. Other Cubans, I suspect, may feel that they too are dangling—that the old ground beneath their feet isn't quite the same.

POST CARD: PRAISE-SONG
FOR OBAMA, PORTUGAL, 2009

I 'M STANDING BEFORE SOME FORTY MEMBERS *of the Faculty of Letters at the University of Coimbra, colleagues from a Fulbright stint in the mid '80s. It's less than two months since Barack Obama took office, and my friends at home are still joyously drinking to his health and our own.*

Obama, I say, with his remarkable history, persona, and special appreciation of American values, is what is new in the United States today. We've elected a black President—the child of a white woman from Kansas and a black African from Kenya—who had the brains and ambition to get into Columbia and Harvard Law, and then did a stint of community organizing. Americans, wearied by Bush's war in Iraq and worried by the collapse of the market, embraced a campaign built around change. *However, Obama's success depended upon rare rhetorical eloquence and a moral vision of America. His own formulation is memorable: "We may have different stories but we hold common hopes. . . . As long as I live, I will never forget that in no other country on Earth is my story possible."*

"Aren't you being naïve?" one colleague asks, opening the door to a barrage of criticism. What will this Democrat do about the war economy,

the power of banks and corporations, the legacy of racism, and the great gap between the Super-rich and other Americans? Indeed, Obama speaks with grace, force, and feeling. But how will those gifts affect legislation? How will he persuade the Congress to raise funds and spend them for health care and education? How will he steady the market?

After the deceptions of the Bush years, I've longed for a smart and trustworthy leader. Now I listen attentively to these Portuguese sceptics, hoping they're wrong.

IN SEARCH OF OAXACAN FOLK ARTS, MEXICO, 2013

A MEXICAN WOMAN BALANCES an enormous fish on her head. A second woman cradles a pre-adolescent boy in one arm and a bunch of carrots almost his size in the other. A third woman carries a tree with a naked Adam and Eve cavorting beneath it. These market women, and six of their *comadres* (none more than five inches tall), sit beneath a banner announcing *Frutas de Ocotlan*. Baskets of gleaming melons, tomatoes, and beans surround the women—along with a pair of tiny turkeys.

This color-drenched, culturally dense market scene occupies a shelf on a bookcase in the front room of my house. What a tribute in clay to the life-giving powers of women! The artist, Josefina Aguilar, is one of four legendary ceramist sisters from Ocotlan de Morelos. All four have produced dazzling work—aided by their husbands and children—for over a half century.

I first visited Ocotlan and other Oaxacan artisan villages in the mid 1990s with my cousin Marlene Kurtz, a Spanish teacher and passionate folk art collector. With her loyal driver, Roberto, my cousin took me to the home-workshops of a dozen of the region's most accomplished artists. At each site, she enthused over the new work, invariably asking about family members and the economic health of the household. She bought boldly and enthusiastically: ceramics, jewelry, weavings, and wood sculpture. I bought modestly: a gorgeously carved alligator, a spotted black cat, and several miniature (six-inch) "ladies of the night." In their skimpy, sparkle-rich attire, the ladies are enjoying a smoke while waiting for business. My favorite, a blonde with large silver earrings and a gold necklace, wears a pink dress, white lace stockings and matching pink flats. She sits with her back very straight on a green chair, pointing defiantly with her cigarette. While the sex/gender system is cruel to these women, Josefina Aguilar has invested them with abundant wit, sass, and a fighting, feminist spirit.

When Marlene died in 2004, I acquired several gems from her collection, including "Frutas de Ocotlan." After the estate sale, some two dozen works languished in cartons in my basement. Then, in 2008, I learned about Friends of Oaxacan Folk Art (FOFA), a small organization of U.S. collectors committed to promoting the traditional arts of Oaxaca. To raise money, FOFA hosts *mescal* parties and sells folk art. I contributed some pieces from Marlene's collection to the cause and attended meetings and fundraisers. In 2013, I flew to Oaxaca with ten other FOFA members to be a part of the organization's second competition for young folk artists. MEAPO (Museo Estadal de Artes Populares de Oaxaca), the sponsoring museum, is a handsome facility located in San Bartolo Coyotepec, about twenty-five minutes from Oaxaca.

ENTERING MEAPO'S SPACIOUS second-floor gallery, I don't know whether to bow, clap, or shout in sheer delight. What a ravishing pastiche of color and form: spiky carved animals, brilliantly painted; tapestries in lush vibrant tones; unlikely constructions of dried red and yellow flowers; and ceramic earth mothers spouting milk or water, embraced by lizards and snakes, adorned by birds, cradling their children.

Tucked among these scene-stealers are quiet treasures: a delicate silver necklace fit to adorn Nefertiti's neck, six narratives of everyday life woven into a slender purse, and a dignified skeletal figure paired with an equally dignified minimalist tree. Ambition and talent, it's quickly apparent, will not be measured simply by scale or visual hoopla.

A hundred and nineteen submissions by young artists (none older than thirty) from the Oaxaca Valley fill the space: clay bowls on white stands of varied heights, carpets and other woven pieces hanging on the barn-red walls, objects of wood and straw on pastel sculpture stands, oversized pieces resting on the black-tiled floor. Mother Earth, the unifying theme, in varied materials, sizes, shapes and colors, is everywhere—celebrated and surprising, often wondrous in form and spirit.

Moving around the gallery, I confront "*La Madre Tierra en su Esplendor*." This woman with an electric, lime-green face is the work of two artists, an eighteen-year-old sculptor and a twenty-five-year-old painter from San Antonio Arazola. Immediately, I announce to the woman standing next to me that I love *La Madre Tierra's* unlovable face, her huge, impeccably rounded, pregnant earth-belly and her globular breasts. I also *really* love the phallic ear of corn, resembling a baby's bottle, which she holds in one hand. The corn, pointing outward, ends in a bright red spot which I *know* to be a nipple. This Earth Mother, with elaborately tattooed arms and legs, is abundantly female and slyly male. The ancient bisexual idea that she embodies resonates loudly in our time.

Who are these savvy artists? I wonder. Young feminists announcing their powers? Internet-inspired post-feminists, borrowing ideas from sci-fi, horror films, and video games? Imagine my shock—and the need to rethink some culturally specific assumptions—when I learn that the sculptor and painter are two guys, brothers.

Taking leave of the woman with the lime-green face, I gravitate toward a simple ceramic piece entitled "Cuidemos a Nuestra Madre Tierra," "Caring for Our Mother Earth," by a ten-year-old artist. Mother Earth weeps. We see her tears; and we see, on either side of her, a girl and a boy offering love and comfort. If I were a *New York Times* critic covering the exhibit, I would want this tender image to illustrate my article. The earth is in trouble, as these young artists know. It is afflicted by pollution, desertification, earthquakes, wildfires, hurricanes, tornados, and floods. What's to be done? How long must we wait? If only our affections were adequate to the challenge.

I join several members of our group who stand transfixed before a ceramic piece, "The Pea Pod," on the human life cycle. Two gray-black pea pods, each about fifteen inches long, with dividers in them, are laid out on a flat surface. At the top of one of the pods sits a fetal figure in off-white clay. Below is a second fetal figure, a child, also in the pod. Outside the second pod, lined up vertically, are three other fetal-like figures: a child, an old man, and a decaying male with a missing leg. What an arresting conception of our time on earth: birth to death in five simplified forms.

Good art is unsettling, uplifting, painful, provocative, and political, too. These young FOFA artists have invested traditional forms with their fears and forebodings, their quirky delights and sense of wonder. I envy their courage, imagination, and skills.

But I don't envy the nine judges (including four Mexicans and two Mexican-Americans) who must choose the best work in ceramics, weaving, wood carving, and painting on carved wood—and the best work by an artist no older than sixteen. At a signal from the lead judge, they all pick up clipboards and paste on neutral expressions. Their decisions will be announced at a public ceremony four days after the judging, on Friday, 9 August.

Fortunately, the exhibition and awards are not the end of the journey for these young artists. Photos of the winning pieces, including many honorable mentions, and statements by the artists about their work, will live on—in an exceptionally handsome, bilingual color catalog published by FOFA and available on its website. In addition, FOFA sponsors short courses, internships, mentoring arrangements, and, on occasion, speaking engagements in the States for a few unusually articulate artists.

I think about Jenifer Garcia Lopez, the ten-year old creator of "Caring for Our Mother Earth" (featured on the cover of the 2013 FOFA catalog). Perhaps, a few years from now, she will be invited to give a talk to folk art *aficionados* in New York or New Jersey. If so, I'll be there, listening. I'll tell Jenifer that I've purchased two copies of her piece, one for myself and the second for my son and his family, who share her passion for honoring and protecting the Earth. Even if Jenifer never makes the trip to *el Norte*, I'll be wondering about her art and her politics. Has she continued working in clay, following in the traditions of Ocotlan, her storied pottery village? Or has she become a landscape artist? An internet designer? An environmentalist? A charismatic organizer for global justice?

POST CARD: HULA IN
HAWAII, 2000–06

ONE AFTERNOON IN HONOLULU, *when I was talking with Japanese and Korean professors about "Diversity in American Life," my stepdaughter Shola went off to the "Kodak Hula Show." A kitschy event, Shola reported, "but an older woman, the queen-pin of the company, put on an astonishing show. She moved effortlessly, taking the edge off her world—and mine." Back in Cambridge, Massachusetts, Shola hunted down a Hula teacher and began taking classes.*

When we started using a time share in Kauai—for a week every other year—Shola found Hula classes for which she paid, as other students did, with canned goods. The work was strenuous, but Shola kept up with the Hawaiians. The teacher, in the spirit of aloha hospitality, asked his assistants, Puamohala and Ka'imilani (sisters), to be attentive to the woman from Massachusetts. At their home, Shola learned new Hula routines; she reciprocated by teaching her hosts Hula steps from her classes in Cambridge.

A couple of years later on Kauai, Shola rejoined the class but found the pace challenging. Puamohala and Ka'imilani, continuing the friendship, invited her home to learn how the dancers' traditional grass skirts are made. "From tree bark— it's sticky, messy work," Shola reported. "Not something an observer would ever know."

Back in Cambridge, Shola sent the Hula teacher and his assistants T-shirts with her own drawing on the front—of the road to the gorgeous Waimea Canyon. Giving and taking across cultures, good travelers know, requires modesty, honesty, and generosity. Hula hooked Shola. She danced through discomfort until one miserable day when a pain in her hip ended the seductive, eight-year adventure. I wonder: Are Mainland hips poorly programmed for Hula? Shola asks, "Is this my punishment for cultural appropriation?"

AMAZING ALASKA, 2015

THE SHIP ROLLS, and I yield to its rhythms. Almost. Perched on my narrow bunk bed, I strain to catch the pink rays disappearing in the distance. Sunset in Alaska at 9:30 p.m. Out of habit, I grab my notebook but quickly put it aside. Not tonight. The magical May light, inky black water, and many sea creatures sighted over the past fifteen hours will have to wait. If I forget, there are always Paul's photos or the photos of our traveling companions for backup. These second-hand prompts, when I'm lucky, can prove more provocative than the real thing: an extra interpretation thrown into the mix of memory and narrative. I'm not a professional nature writer, I remind myself: just a tourist with permission to bask in visual overload. Lindblad Expeditions, in collaboration with National Geographic, has promised no less: two exceptional weeks on the *Sea Lion*, a small, comfortable ship cruising from Seattle north to Glacier Bay National Park.

It's time now to let go: throw a kiss to Paul in the bunk bed perpendicular to mine and embrace sweet sleep. Waves, mounting a minor military campaign, Paul reports the next morning, exploded repeatedly against the window next to my bed. I was otherwise occupied, I tell him—sunbathing with sea lions and dancing with Spirit Bears.

Credit for such blissful sleep belongs to the great outdoors: sun, cool air (temperatures between forty and fifty degrees), and constant wind. With hats and sunscreen for protection, we're out there for some part of each day: kayaking, cruising around in rubber Zodiacs (light-weight motorized boats holding ten people), or walking on hilly terrain. Occasionally, we get a close-up look at a glacier about to calve: a vast slice of ice, separating from "the parent," global warming in action. Sometimes, when the Zodiac approaches a narrow beach, we wade ashore in tall rubber boots for a half-hour nature walk. "Smell the bear shit," our guide David says, as I'm about to slip on the stuff. "It's fresh and clean."

In the dining room and the ship's lounge—with forty-two other travelers and our team of naturalists and professional photographers—we eat simply and drink moderately. The lunch buffet always includes a big salad and fresh fruit. Evenings, I limit myself to one stiff Johnny Walker during the cocktail hour and one glass of sauvignon blanc with a healthy, American-style dinner: fresh vegetables, potatoes or rice, along with roast chicken, broiled fish, or lightly-sauced meat. Our companions at the table—like us, of retirement age (even if still working) and well-traveled—also welcome the unfussy cuisine.

The ship's routines free us to look and help us to see. Our four naturalists offer lively lectures on sea life, resourceful animals, and native cultures. Each of the professional photographers gives a pre-dinner presentation of his or her own work; these include pointing out weaknesses in particular shots and how they might have been improved. They spend time with passengers discussing better use of equipment, framing the image, and managing the light. The naturalists and the photographers all seem to relish recycling instructive moments from other trips. Their pleasure in this work is contagious; we benefit from their experience, abundant good humor, and straight talk.

Our route, through the inland waterways of southern British Columbia and then into southern Alaska, offers at least fifty enticing photographic opportunities per minute. I say this as someone who religiously travels "camera free" and buys scenic postcards. I'll also enjoy the best among thousands of photos taken by everyone in our group except for one literary couple and an enthusiastic blind man, born sighted, who seems, magically, to see it all.

For three provocative days at Haida Gwaii, we listen to Native guides explain their community's history and culture, beginning at the Museum and Haida Heritage Center. We follow them from one famous thirty-foot totem pole to another, sometimes catching a Haida sculptor's explanation of the design of his pole or a friend's pole. One guide, commenting on clan warfare, celebrates leaders in his lineage who survive due to wit, generosity, and enlightenment. (I'm jealous. What American in my circle in 2016 might make such a statement?) How many people does it take to raise a thirty-foot pole? someone asks. "One hundred, if we're lucky," the guide responds. "But it could be up to four hundred."

Interruptions belong to the rhythm. When the announcement *Sea Lions on starboard* is made, our gang of forty-four passengers abandons the luncheon table and races up to the deck. Directly in front of us on a rocky outcropping are some seventy sea lions (sexually exhausted males, we're told), lying back, nuzzling one another. They moan loudly, flap around, sigh, absorb the sun, and seem absurdly contented.

At other moments our guides point out pods of killer whales rising out of the water and diving back in; also, ospreys and sandpipers, puffins and ravens, pelicans and loons. Occasionally, a sparkling white mountain goat, as if fresh from the dry cleaners, peeks out from the forested hillside.

"Keep the talk down," Larry says. "The water amplifies your voices. You'll scare him away." Our lead naturalist is giving wise advice to a gang of us leaning far over the rails, most with cameras and binoculars dangling. We're watching a black bear emerge from hiding—from a site fifteen hundred feet high, partly covered with dense yellow cedar. It's 2:00 p.m. and surprisingly warm. Paul has stripped down to his shirt sleeves, and I've liberated myself from a loose wool hat that keeps slipping over my forehead, blocking my view. The air is still, and the sky is French Impressionist blue.

The bear has us transfixed. Will he move right or left, slowly or quickly, and in response to what provocations? My companions' shutters keep clicking. They're on their toes, bodies extended, precariously balanced. Are they pressing to get The Perfect Photo? Or is something larger at stake? Some wish to connect with Nature's Beast? With his capacity for destruction? Or the delusion that, if approached correctly, the bear might kick a soccer ball or do a little jig? The beast interests me less than the passion he stirs in my companions.

About half-way up the rock face, to the left of the bear's hiding place, wind, water, and time have carved a pair of fat human lips surrounding a circular, open mouth. Have I seen that shape in Bill Holm's remarkable book on Haida art? On a totem pole in Alert Bay? Or on one of the three dozen postcards that I've been collecting at small museums and gift shops? I'm not sure which is more amazing: what Nature does, or how Experience shapes what and how we see.

The announcement comes at lunch: "We have a real treat for this afternoon. Once each voyage, we offer an Arctic plunge. Guests wishing to experience these waters in May will jump or dive off a raft attached to the ship and then swim thirty feet to another waiting raft. We'll have towels ready, and we'll bring you back to a cheering audience. No pressure. No heroics. Just a jump and a swim."

As someone who wants the water in her swimming pool to be no less than eighty degrees, I don't give a minute's thought to the Plunge. It would take my body a week to recover. At 3:00 p.m., about a dozen people in bathing suits line up at the ship's stern, to be loaded into the plunge raft. Paul, as it turns out, is the only male in the group. He stands out in the hundreds of Plunge pics as the one with a bare top and rotund middle.

ON THE AFTERNOON OF DAY #12 at Glacier Bay, Kim Heacox joins our group. Heacox is a Park Service officer, a naturalist and a writer. A small, soft-spoken man, he arrives with two cartons of books, including many of his own. After Larry introduces him,

Heacox wastes no time getting into his subject: America's wilderness heritage is under attack from climate change and ever-encroaching capitalism. The National Park Service, he surprises us by announcing, is all that stands between "our glorious heritage" and ruin.

I buy Heacox's "midlife memoir," *The Only Kayak: A Journey into the Heart of Alaska*. The book, I quickly discover, is a twenty-first century *Walden Pond*: a symphony to the wonders of the natural world, a psychology primer, and a political broadside. Nature, as Heacox knows from twenty-five years in Glacier Bay, is not a benign god. Nature challenges even those who study it well and venerate its powers. One of his closest friends, Heacox writes, was killed by a bear at Glacier Bay. The friend, a professional photographer and frequent visitor to Alaska, had camped alone in an isolated spot. Tragedy, Heacox comments, teaches the need to respect the unknowable.

In choosing to travel on a small, ecologically alert ship like the *Sea Lion*, we make our political statement. Let us help preserve the wilderness for Native peoples, for sea life and wildlife, and for our grandchildren to enjoy. But often enough, we catch sight of monstrous tourist ships—those floating twenty-story buildings with multiple movie theaters and pools, with a track, an armada of stationary bikes and a climbing wall; with saunas, steam rooms, and a choice of internet cafes. On board and relishing all the comforts of home are the oilmen, the wood-to-paper plutocrats, and the shopping mall developers. (If any of those folks are on the *Sea Lion*, they're keeping an under-the-rug profile.) Who will protect the remaining tidewater glaciers from the Demons of Development?

Who will manage the garbage? And how? Alaska, amazing Alaska, is at risk, Heacox makes clear. Make access easy, he writes, and a place will die. "Access becomes excess."

POST CARD: BRINGING NEWS
OF 9/11, POLAND, 2011

I DIDN'T THINK I WOULD GET HERE," *I tell a lecture hall full of Polish professors of American literature and American history. While thirty-six days have passed since 9/11, my friends and I still see the smoke, or think we do, from the fallen Towers. We're still in a fog of mourning for the five thousand dead, victims of attacks by Islamist terrorists on the World Trade Center and the Pentagon.*

A cartoon in the New York Times *(September 30, 2001) by Michael Thompson captures the occasion. At the airport, a soldier confronts a frenetic woman passenger. She's clutching a pocketbook in one hand and a suitcase in the other. "Where do you wish to travel," the soldier asks.*

"September 10," she responds.

I know this traveler, and I know what she feels. September 10, the last day of our seeming innocence and safety, is the destination we all dream of returning to.

I remember on 9/11 the dozens of fire trucks assembled in the Meadowlands between Leonia and Teaneck, about five minutes from my house, preparing to fight the fires in Lower Manhattan. The tears came as I drove past that sunny field, glimpsing volunteers pulling on slickers and masks, pushing aside thoughts of their wives and children and ambitions for the future. The emergency defined them: terror on our shores, innocent workers trapped in their offices, on coffee breaks or heading for an early lunch.

While nothing is as it was, much remains unchanged. We Americans must reckon with our government's economic and military policies, our place in the global order, and threats from Islamist terrorists. How I wish we could simply gather with friends, order in pizza, and drink lots of wine.

XANDARI: TORRENTIAL RAINS AND TREES LIKE CATHEDRALS, COSTA RICA, 2017

PAUL TALKS TO BIRDS. In many languages. He tweets, hoots, whistles, and experiments with plosives. The smartest among them talk back. Unless they're just doing what birds do: sounding off to mate, eat, and protect their turf. Paul knows this and plays to their strengths. Or to his own—as a man of a certain age without other spoken foreign languages. Here in Tropical Costa Rica, where hummingbirds flourish and vultures feast, where the wise owl presides and the yellow-throated euphonia makes a billboard appearance, Paul is in his own linguistic heaven.

I don't do birds. Spanish, my challenge of choice in this part of the world, keeps me occupied. On a good day, the many words forgotten are offset by phrases unexpectedly remembered. At age eighty, I'm on the down side of the learning equation but still smooth enough to collect compliments. "I've been speaking Spanish for more than fifty years," I explain to Jose, our Costa Rican waiter, "for more than fifty years, and besides, *Nueva York es una ciudad bilingual.*" Vanity prevents me from acknowledging that my beginnings *en Espanol* go back *sixty* years. Sixty-one to be exact, to my first year in college.

I do rhapsodize about flowers—especially the magnificent heliconia. "Get that one on film," I tell Paul, pointing to a striking bird-like variety—red with green-yellow tips, about six feet tall and often growing in clusters of a dozen or more. Sometimes, the "birds" appear to be grabbing a nap in the sun; at other times, they seem poised to take flight—or move heavenward. Heliconia, one of the chatty landscapers tells me, "*son especial, casi divino.*" They're named after Mount Helicon, the seat of the Muses, I discover. They're also exported to the U.S., like papayas and bananas. Perhaps I can buy heliconia at Metropolitan Plants in Fort Lee, New Jersey. If so, will they appear glorious on my coffee table? Or sadly domesticated and diminished?

June in Costa Rica is the winter season, with temperatures ranging from 50 to 90 degrees Fahrenheit. Reliably, each day's drama revolves around The Deluge. Will it arrive at midday, at mid-afternoon, or in early evening? Our hotel, Xandari, located in Alajuela between Costa Rica's two popular coasts, occupies forty acres of a former coffee plantation. We worry. Will we be caught—trapped or assaulted—while prowling the gorgeously landscaped grounds? In the hot tub? On our way to dinner? Without an oversized, world-class umbrella, which Xandari provides for guests, we are helpless—like Noah without an ark. In this weather, the lightweight folding devices we've packed resemble children's toys.

Costa Ricans refuse to fuss about The Deluge. They notice when it arrives later than usual or is more benign than usual.

Mostly, they appreciate the relation between tropical rain and their prized abundance: bananas, mangoes, papayas, and oranges. These export crops—along with tropical flowers and no military force—keep the national budget in balance.

Xandari does fuss about its locally grown fruits and vegetables. Guests are encouraged to visit the extensive vegetable garden—less than ten minutes down the hill from the main building; and we are expected to gape at the eye-level stand of hydroponic lettuces and herbs positioned just a few feet from the entrance to the dining room. "Tonight's salad," one of the workers says as he snips a selection of dewy greens, tosses them into a straw basket, and heads for the kitchen. My favorite breakfast treat (a feature of the Farm-to-Table menu) is the House Five-Star Fruit Juice: a pale green blend of locally grown kale with pineapple, orange juice, honey, and sugar. Take note, Whole Foods! You can make headlines with this drink! And a modest killing, too.

Fowl, featured on lunch and dinner menus, are locally raised. The birds, Josefina informs us at dinner, welcome visitors to their open Hen House during daylight hours. Signs indicating *.25 miles* show portraits of "Hansel and Gretel," the proud turkey and sociable chicken, awaiting us. Accustomed to human company, they chirp as we approach.

While there's so much drama out of doors, Xandari's twenty-four oversized units are a destination in themselves. Our brilliantly painted blue-and-white space has separate areas for sleeping, reading, chatting, snacking, and writing. The woven rugs and playful abstract prints show off the owner's (and designer's) sophisticated taste. From our large terrace, we enjoy views of rolling fields, fruit trees, and manic bird doings. Opposite the terrace, large screened doors open onto a densely planted private inner garden. A luxury touch—just like the shower that's built to hold a family. When the Deluge arrives, we relish the down-time.

AT BREAKFAST ON OUR FINAL TUESDAY morning, at our corner table on the terrace facing the green hills, we are greeted by a regimen of flies. I've barely gotten started on my kale juice and am unprepared for what seems like a state visit. The word is out that we are leaving, and our winged friends have come to say *adios*.

In a few minutes, our taxi will arrive and we'll be performing our farewells. Farewell to the deep green banana plants, the bamboo cathedral, the heliconias masquerading as birds, and the lipstick palms. Farewell to ten miles of carefully curated walks, three lap pools (each with a different temperature) and three always-empty outdoor hot tubs. Farewell to "Hansel and Gretel" and their family of edible creatures.

A special good-bye to Jose and Josefina and the spirited bilingual staff. Day after day, they receive us enthusiastically, gabbing with me in Spanish and switching smoothly into English with Paul. In the dining room, wherever we sit, a member of the wait staff remembers that Chilean Aromo is our sauvignon blanc of choice. We'll miss our huge terrace and interior garden, Paul and I say, almost in the same instant: especially the two walls of windows for viewing the daily tropical dramas from either the bed or the sofa.

"But wait, there's a special farewell gift we have for you," the young manager announces. "Give me a minute. I need to see our chef." Less than ten minutes later, he appears with a half dozen chocolate-covered strawberries, trimmed with white chocolate, each on a stick resting in a small pineapple base. Our own Xandari *arbol*. "*Muy rica,*" the manager says.

"*Y tan elegante,*" I respond. I don't let on that the treat is much *too* rich for our morning appetites.

The taxi is waiting, and we pile in with our bags and our strawberries. On the way the airport, Paul and I devour three of the six goodies. Even better than advertised! Before we climb out of the taxi, I offer the remaining three, in their pineapple stand, to the driver. "My wife will be so delighted," he responds.

"*Me allegro,*" I say, "but please don't mention this to the management."

POST CARD: SMITTEN BY
A "LAST SUPPER," PORTUGAL, 1985

FROM MY OFFICE ON THE SIXTH FLOOR *of the Faculty of Let-*
ters, I look down on Coimbra's famous Machado de Castro (State)
Museum. Some days I spot Eli in his jeans and scruffy jeans jacket about
to enter the courtyard. He's been haunting the place since we arrived in
January, when he first encountered a Last Supper by the sixteenth-cen-
tury French sculptor Phillipe Hodart.

This Last Supper, Eli reports, is "a paraplegic ward"—arms and legs
are missing, and bodies shattered. What remains are a series of remarkably
expressive terra cotta heads of Christ and his disciples, organized around
a long stone table. Broken figures with manic energy! He mentions sweet
John, moody Judas, the Apostle with his mouth open—saying what?—
and a radiant, regal Christ.

Newly retired, Eli is ready for Hodart. He plunges into accounts
of sixteenth-century French artists, along with Medieval, Renaissance,
and Baroque art. He interviews curators and art historians. Nothing is
known about the sculptor's origins—only that he is French. Eli wonders
who modeled for the apostles, what space the work originally occupied,
and why it was destroyed. As a painter, he admires the psychological re-

alism of these portraits—deep feelings conveyed by a glance, grimace, or gesture. He knows the effort and imagination required to invest his own figurative paintings with a similar richness.

Hodart provokes Eli and interferes with his sleep. The dead artist joins us at breakfast, and sometimes over drinks with colleagues. It's "creative combat," Eli says, an invaluable retirement gift to himself. When we leave Coimbra in June, Eli takes Hodart with him. It will be another two years before his essay, "Resurrecting Phillipe Hodart," appears in The Massachusetts Review.

STICKY RICE—TOURISTS AND TRAFFIC, VIETNAM, 2018

S TICKY RICE," HUY ANNOUNCES over the Whisperer. I caress the small device hanging on a lanyard around my neck and check my left earplug. It's in place. I'm connected. No need to panic—not as long as I can hear our guide's calm voice and reassuring instructions.

The tour bus has deposited our group of seventeen travelers "across the street," some might say, from the War Remnants Museum. In New York terms, we're a land-mine away: i.e., five lanes of traffic between the bus and museum, unregulated by traffic lights. "Stay close together," Huy cautions us. "Make no sudden moves. Follow my signals."

This flood of traffic moving through the center city—generally five lanes each way, three for motorbikes and two for cars—has no American equivalent. Venturing across on my own, I might as well be walking on my hands on overheated tar. Listening to Huy, I stop obsessing about burned palms and broken bones. I take a deep breath and grab Paul's arm as we move forward.

Bizarre traffic patterns overwhelm American and European

visitors to Vietnam. How could they not? Yet during almost three weeks with the *Nation* tour, negotiating Ho Chi Minh City, Hanoi, and four other busy smaller cities, we've seen few accidents. Correction—we haven't seen a single instance of a car or motorbike hitting a *pedestrian*—or a pedestrian who has been hit. Vietnamese drivers, it would appear, are a different breed from ours: They move in a steady rhythm with others, rarely breaking out of the pack. Most motorbikes (Vespa scooters are common) carry two passengers, often with a child between them, occasionally with two children. Drivers appear attentive but not visibly tense. They go with the flow; they don't honk, show anger, or make obscene gestures. What's more, we see no car collisions and few battered cars or bikes. Even bulky tour buses, negotiating tight parking lots, seem (miraculously) unscarred.

Public transportation, as best I can tell, is under-developed in these cities. The Japanese, rumor has it, are building a subway here. Along the major avenues, sidewalks double as parking lots for motorbikes. Walking in the city, as we know it, seems confined to local neighborhoods with narrow streets, or to some glitzy, tourist-jammed blocks loaded with restaurants, coffee shops, fruit sellers, and stores that will make a jacket or dress to size in less than six hours.

I've always thought of myself, to borrow Alfred Kazin's term, as "a walker in the city." Growing up on the Upper West Side of Manhattan in a family without a car, I valued walking—as a way of knowing my neighborhood and borough, and of tracking cultural changes as reflected on the street. Vivian Gornick's recent memoir, *The Odd Woman and the City,* underscores the idea of New York as best known by those who encounter it up close and on foot.

Still, I remind myself that walking my city is losing its magic. Delivery trucks, bikers, construction machinery, blocks torn up for months on end, tons of uncollected garbage in plastic bags, pedestrians attentive only to their smart phones, rudeness, aggressive driving, and road rage all compromise the city I'm happy to have left—more than forty years ago—for the suburbs. But still. In New York, there are traffic lights, and they work. They even tell the pedestrian how many seconds she has to cross six lanes of cars, trucks, buses, and an occasional biker on Upper Broadway.

Two days earlier, at Hotel La Caravelle in Ho Chi Minh City, Paul and I sat in front of a wall of windows facing the old French Opera House. Sun filled the plaza. Two Vinasun taxis entered the side street and parked less than thirty feet from where we sat. Both drivers—wearing red ties to match the red line on their cabs—got out, stretched their arms and backs, and settled themselves on a nearby bench. We watched as a woman in high heels on a motorbike adjusted her helmet; and another, seated behind her companion, adjusted her face mask. (At least thirty percent of bikers use masks. Many Vietnamese, mostly women, wear them all day long.) Sipping cappuccinos, we observed an elegant young woman in a long peach gown, and her companion in a pale beige suit, being photographed in front of the Opera House. Were they a wedding couple about to marry? Models posing for a *Vogue* ad—or for a *New York Times* special section on Travel in Asia? The real story wasn't important—only the tranquil bar from which to view the action without palpitations.

In Vietnam, I'm obsessed by the Culture of Traffic. The movement, all day long, of car drivers, cabbi``es, and motor-bikers—without honking, angry gestures, or accidents—underscores cultural ideals of harmony and self-restraint, on the one hand, and energetic living on the other. Young Vietnamese—ages twenty to forty-five—seem focused, self-controlled, and confident. Like Huy, they're "boomers," born after the trauma of war and after the suffering of their grandparents and parents (from American military aggression). The past, for them, is past. Americans are welcome in their midst. Even the dreams of Chairman Ho's communism have been radically altered to stimulate growth, profit-making, and world-class development. The young people in these ten lanes of traffic belong to the prosperous present and the even more promising future. They are dressed, most of them, for business—slacks and jackets for men; skirts or slacks, often with dress shoes, for women. In due course, they will shift into warm-ups and gym clothes. Soon enough, I'm guessing, but not quite yet.

While functioning in the fast lane, these Vietnamese have not thrown caution to the wind. On the contrary, they seem to have found a balance that eludes us. I think back to our tour guide's instructions and the wisdom they contain—especially as he urged us to stay in a group, close together, even though that's not our inclination nor our habit. "Sticky rice," Huy's metaphor for group behavior, suggests modesty, restraint, collective support, imagination sacrificed to responsibility. His lessons for survival—in Vietnam—haunt me. In a dream several days before leaving, a member of our group with an injured leg clings to me as we're crossing the avenue. I pull away. Sticky rice, the dream suggests, can't be learned in a fortnight. In any case, I'm probably too old for cross-cultural education. Or too selfish. Or too stubbornly American.

POST CARD: AT THE DMZ, KOREA, 2002

F ROM SEOUL, WHERE I'VE BEEN ATTENDING *a conference on Feminist Studies and English Literature, I take a tourist bus thirty-five miles to the DMZ. It's an easy ride, less than an hour, to the famously enigmatic borderland. We've all been instructed to bring our passports.*

A South Korean military officer in fatigues addresses our group of eight. The DMZ, he tells us, is four kilometers (two and a half miles) wide. "You'll see barbed wire fences for the entire 250-kilometer (155-mile) length of the zone. Stay away from them." As he speaks, loudspeakers from the North, emitting a whooshing sound, bombard us with indecipherable messages: PR, I assume, for their Noble Nation and Magnificent Leader.

I'm struck, even in this din, by something extraordinary: Our guide, the fellow in fatigues, is speaking flawless American English. Like a New Yorker! A few minutes later, when I compliment him on his mastery of my mother tongue, he tells me that he graduated from Paramus Catholic—a high school about twelve minutes from my home. "And you?" he asks. "Where are you from?"

When I mention Leonia, he says he has cousins there, on Lakeview

Avenue. *Lakeview,* I say, crosses *Hillcrest,* my street. "I see *Lakeview* from my front door."

Later that day, at the bar in my hotel, I describe this encounter to a woman from San Francisco. As soon as I begin speaking, I realize that I never asked the soldier his name—or the name of his relatives on *Lakeview.* Since my town is twenty-five percent Asian, I'm not likely to find them on my own.

AIRPORTS ARE FOR WAITING
AND OTHER CONCLUSIONS

J*ET* B*LUE* *FLIGHT* #*202* *TO* S*AN* F*RANCISCO has been delayed due to heavy winds in the Bay Area. We do apologize for this inconvenience. My name is Sherry Riley, and I'm here at the boarding gate. If I can be of help to any of you, please see me. Again, Jet Blue apologizes for this delay.*

Sherry Riley's voice is loud and clear. And irritating—perhaps because she has made this announcement three times in the last ten minutes. Thanks, Jet Blue, for the apologies, for the niceties of Air-Speak; thanks for keeping passengers (I keep wanting to say "patients") informed, mollified, and well-disposed to the airline. I feel the commercial driving the information. "We're here for you, doing our best. Stay with us. You won't be sorry."

Wait a minute. Am I actually expecting an on-time departure? We travelers are accustomed to waiting. We are accustomed to zoning out—and tuning out—even when we can't help hearing the auditory assault. Large overhead TVs, positioned every fifty feet or so, feature the latest air crash and domestic shooting; they zero in on the American leader with the long red tie who's about to make a statement. At home I tune him out, but here in the airport, there's no escaping his posturing, blather, and lies.

Yes, we are accustomed to being targeted—as opposed to chasing bargains and saving a few bucks at Target. We're accustomed to inconvenience, ritualized apologies, lining up too soon, tolerating ever more Service Animals (some for people who appear able-bodied) and less and less Service.

Traveling, we entertain ourselves at the Airport as Mall. For Americans, at least, at a moment when malls are being replaced by online shopping, airports conjure up familiar territory—along with multiple opportunities to actually examine the goods one will buy. Shopping blunts our anxieties with an array of name-brand collectibles, pointless mementos, and bargain booze at the duty free. I note Paul's delight in buying at least one bottle of expensive Scotch—adding weight and bulk as we deplane—even though discount liquor dealers, a mere ten minutes from home, do almost as well.

The airport is Big Brand Territory. From McDonald's and Dunkin' Donuts to Starbucks and Legal Seafood, familiar names beckon. Just like on the expressway. Knowing what we're getting is one kind of come-on. Exotic opportunities are another. We can choose A or B—or with enough time to kill, A *and* B. Restaurants (and some bars) seduce us with ethnic variety and menus ranging from ham and cheese to *fromage* and *charcuterie*. Paella prepares us for Spain, Poke for Hawaii, and couscous for the Middle East and North Africa. Eating in the right frame of mind, we're already in flight.

I watch a blonde woman with long legs in expensive leather boots set herself up for waiting. Placing her carry-on about a foot from her feet, she opens her laptop on her lap and settles a small shopping bag on the next seat. From the bag, she pulls out a salad, a small muffin, and a bottle of water. Without missing a beat, she lifts her legs onto the carry-on, removes her light blazer, opens the plastic salad container and digs into her greens. Gotta be kale, I'm thinking. Trendy and healthy and tasty enough, I'll bet, especially with a Caesar dressing.

Few travelers have it so easy. An elderly woman with an un-smiling aide looks around anxiously for someone to watch their bags while the two of them visit the rest room. A man four seats down from the blonde hisses into his phone in Russian, twisting and turning as he talks. Is he afraid of being overheard—or looking for a connection? A pair of five-year-olds dash past the Russian speaker, almost banging into the beige leather bag at his feet as their mother nervously looks on. At least they're not hitting one another, she's probably thinking, or shouting. . .or wanting more soft ice cream. They shared (most of) a Softee about fifteen minutes ago before one of the kids ran head-first into the mom, and the dish slipped from her hands.

The manic five-year-olds remind me of the innocent-looking blond child in Eli's 1988 oil titled *Terrorist at Heathrow*. (Note: *Terrorist* was completed three years before 9/11, and 9/11 occurred three months after Eli's death.) We glimpse the child hiding with his toy gun behind a bank of red plastic chairs. Restless while waiting, he amuses himself as little boys do, as they've learned from older men. The painting, with its blend of mischief and menace, reminds us that appearances are deceiving. Are we confronting "a bad seed" or a costumed, post-modern child? Or neither? More than ever since 9/11, we look with suspicion at those around us—especially at those who are different from us; we speculate and stereotype, imagining attacks being planned and destruction in the wings.

Still, we are not hiding at home. A powerful nor'easter can leave us disabled tomorrow; a guy with three guns can shoot us at Shop Rite. So why not take our chances? The airport will be plastic and junk-laden, an assault on our ears and our sensibilities. However, the delayed plane, when it finally departs, will probably be faster (and safer) than those we took ten years ago. We'll travel, feeling more anxious than we care to admit, because we have the habit, the ridiculous dreams, and the dollars. We'll travel knowing that waiting is familiar and normal: woven into the fabric of aging, which we fend off by staying in motion.

ABOUT THE AUTHOR

Doris Friedensohn is Professor Emerita of Women's Studies at New Jersey City University. She holds a B.A. from Barnard College, and an M.A. and Ph.D. in American Studies from Yale University. A former Vice President of the American Studies Association (ASA), Friedensohn chaired the Women's Committee of the Association, served on the International Committee, and traveled widely on behalf of American Studies. She has written on food and contemporary American culture, U.S. diversity, feminist pedagogy, and doing American Studies abroad. The American Studies Association's Bode Pearson Prize, which she was awarded in 2003, acknowledges a lifetime of achievement and service in the field.